Pursuing Justice in a Sinful World

STEPHEN V. MONSMA

WILLIAM B. EERDMANS PUBLISHING COMPANY
GRAND RAPIDS, MICHIGAN

To Richard L. Stravers,
who pursued justice with me

Copyright © 1984 by William B. Eerdmans Publishing Co.
255 Jefferson Ave. S.E., Grand Rapids, Mich. 49503
Printed in the United States of America

Library of Congress Cataloging in Publication Data

Monsma, Stephen V., 1936-
Pursuing justice in a sinful world.

1. Christianity and politics. I. Title.
BR115.P7M556 1984   261.7   84-13784

ISBN 0-8028-0023-8 (pbk.)

CONTENTS

PREFACE

In *Mere Christianity* C. S. Lewis writes about "a civil war, a rebellion" raging in the universe, with our earth being "enemy-occupied territory." This war is between the fallen angel Satan, an evil power who "has made himself for the present the Prince of this World," and God, who created this world good and beautiful. "Christianity," Lewis goes on to say, "is the story of how the rightful king has landed . . . and is calling us all to take part in a great campaign of sabotage" (Macmillan, pp. 36, 37).

This book is about the war of sabotage Christ and his children are waging against the dark power of this world in a particular institutional setting: politics. It is about a war, about a struggle for Christ's justice in a world too often dominated by the pride and the selfishness that are the stock-in-trade of the dark forces of evil.

For ten years, as a candidate for public office and as a state legislator, I have been directly and personally involved in this struggle—too often in a hesitant, fumbling manner, yet hopefully more often than not on the side of our Lord's justice. For this reason this book is highly personal. It is about principles—about justice—but throughout I see them through the lenses of my own experiences.

Since this book is rooted in my years of experience in politics, I need to pause to give thanks to those who gave me crucial help in my political career: to Leanne Van Dyk and Susanne Van Dyk (now Susanne Jordan), who spent endless hours compiling lists for my first successful campaign for the Michigan House of Representatives; to Dick Klaver, Carolyn Brock, David Medema, Patricia Holden-Myatt, Elizabeth Garcia, Tom Tobin, Lee Hobrla, and Kris Pilon, whose work on my legislative staff reflected their own pursuits of justice; to my many friends at Calvin College and the Church of the Servant, who supported me with prayers, time, and contributions; and to my wife, Mary, and two children, Martin and Kristin, to whom my pursuit of justice usually translated into nothing more glamorous than an absent husband and father. Finally, I wish especially to thank Rick Stravers, who for four years pursued justice with me as a member of my legislative staff and whose perspectives and thoughts are reflected throughout this book.

Pursuing Justice
in a
Sinful World

1

THE CHALLENGE

As a Michigan state legislator I once introduced a package of bills aimed at getting drunk drivers off the road. The chances of its passing had looked good. Then another legislator, who had earlier introduced his own drunk-driving bill, claimed jurisdiction to all drunk-driving legislation and committed himself to blocking my bills. But I was equally committed to opposing his bill, since everyone associated with the issue acknowledged it would do next to nothing.

The majority leader called us both into his office to try to break the impasse. Things soon degenerated into a shouting match, with the other legislator using a string of profanities to insist that it was going to be his bill or nothing at all, and loudly telling me where I could go. I, with equal heat, insisted that I was not going to tolerate the passage of a sham bill. I got up to leave, and our shouting continued out into the hallway. Finally, the majority leader got us back into his office and negotiated an agreement that resulted—for all intents and purposes—in the other legislator backing off and my bills being the ones that were put in line for passage.

This time I had won. But my nerves were frayed and I felt physically drained from the intense negotiations and the profane verbal abuse that I had been subjected to.

As I walked back to my office with my aide—who, like me, is an evangelical Christian—I said to him with a wry smile, "Isn't it great to be pursuing justice in a sinful world?"

"Well," he replied, "it's a sinful world, all right!"

That single incident illustrates much of what this book is about. The legislation that I was struggling for was of crucial importance and was fully in keeping with the highest ideals of justice. Nearly eight hundred persons are killed every year in Michigan alone in alcohol-related accidents. A personal friend of mine had recently been hit and permanently injured by a drunk driver who earlier had killed someone else while driving drunk. Yet society's attitudes and our laws both proclaim that drunk driving is really not a serious offense. I am certain that the senseless, useless carnage we allow to continue on our highways is an offense to our Lord. His justice demands better of us.

It was out of this sense of moral outrage that I, along with others, became involved in the issue of drunk-driving legislation. The bills we drafted were eventually enacted into law, and Michigan now has some of the toughest drunk-driving statutes in the nation. Justice was done. But the process of getting these bills enacted into law was difficult, agonizing, and in some ways even sordid. The goals of the bills and the ideals that motivated my pressing for their passage were rooted in God's revealed Word; the process of pushing them through the legislature was seemingly totally removed from the world of ideals and justice.

It is always so in the political world. Politics—rightly understood and rightly practiced—deals with concepts of righteousness and justice. But it does not deal with them in the abstract. It seeks to take these ideals and apply them in a tough world marked by struggle and combat.

THE WORLD OF IDEALS AND
THE WORLD OF PRACTICE

My own life has spanned both the world of theory and the world of active political involvement. I taught political science for ten years, seven of them at an evangelical Christian college. I have written a book and several articles in which I have argued for applying the biblical ideals of justice and righteousness in politics.

For the last ten years I have been deeply involved in the political arena. During this time I have been a candidate for the Michigan state legislature four times and a candidate for the United States Congress once. I have spent four years in the Michigan House of Representatives and four years in the Michigan Senate,* and now serve on Michigan's Natural Resources Commission.

I have found that the world of ideas and ideals is not only relevant to the real political world; it is indispensable to effective, purposeful action in it. Though obviously different, the two worlds are connected—they need each other. It is something like the relationship between sitting by a cozy fire in your living room on a cold winter's evening with the seed catalog before you, planning which luscious-looking fruits and vegetables and which lovely flowers you are going to grow in your garden next summer, and actually going out into the garden, getting dirt under your fingernails, pulling weeds, and fighting off insects. The two worlds are more than related: they are essential to each other. No garden can be made to produce without thinking and planning. But neither can a garden be made to produce without one's getting down on one's knees in the dirt under a hot sun and doing the difficult, sweaty work. Similarly, effective, meaningful Christian political involvement requires not only ideals and visions but also a willingness to get dirt under one's fingernails out in the real political world. And the real political world is indeed a tough, risky, sweaty place.

In his book *Between a Rock and a Hard Place* (Word, 1976), United States Senator Mark Hatfield has graphically described the lack of ideals in the real political world:

> Such ideals are, for all practical purposes, disregarded. At best, they form stirring rhetoric for speeches to constituents. Rarely are they what move men and women to seek and preserve political power.
>
> A facade of statesmanlike idealism conceals a brothel of egomania and lust for power which prostitutes those in political life for often nothing more than personal vain-glory. (p. 21)

---

*Michigan has a full-time legislature, which means that for eight years holding public office was my full-time occupation.

Confronting this reality had led Hatfield to seriously consider not running for reelection to the Senate: "I was sick and tired of this all that day, five years ago, and countless other days before and since then. As the plane climbed out of Washington, I was relieved. I had little desire to return" (p. 21).

To bring the world of Christian ideals to bear on national and international needs in today's political arena is a constant, frustrating, debilitating struggle. Hatfield is not the only Christian political officeholder who has nearly given up.

Both the world of ideals and the world of practical, day-to-day political action are necessary and important. But they need to be brought together, not kept in separate compartments. Thus this book is about the pursuit of justice; it is about ideals and visions. But it is also about pursuing justice in a sinful— even sordid—world.

EVANGELICAL POLITICAL AND SOCIAL INVOLVEMENT

The evangelical church seems to be more comfortable with and more involved in the world of ideas and ideals than in the world of politics. This is understandable, and it's not all bad. If anything, Christians need to do more rather than less thinking about what the biblical calls to "seek justice" and to "defend the cause of the fatherless, plead the case of the widow" mean in the final decades of the twentieth century.

But neither is it by any means all good. Christians need to take the insights of biblical Christianity out into the world— including the political world—so that their power to have a positive, constructive effect on our society and its hurts can be unleashed. Fortunately, it is becoming increasingly clear that, following a period of withdrawal from political and social involvement, evangelical Christians are regaining this vision of applying their faith to social and political ills.

In the past, committed, biblical Christians were often in the forefront of social and political change. In seventeenth-century England it was the Puritans who overthrew the monarchy in a movement that Georgia Harkness in her book on John

4

Calvin described as "a political movement of which the inception and chief dynamic lay in the area of religion." In late eighteenth-century England the Clapham Sect, a group of evangelical Christians led by William Wilberforce, played the major role in abolishing the English slave trade and worked for other progressive social reforms. In the nineteenth century American evangelicals were very active in movements for prohibition and women's rights and against slavery and poverty. They organized protest rallies, led marches, engaged in civil disobedience, and outraged polite society.

But in the early decades of the twentieth century, American evangelicals tended, for a variety of reasons, to withdraw from social and political involvement. They developed instead a subculture that existed separate from the mainstream of American society and its social and political issues.

But now this is changing. American evangelicals are once again becoming socially and politically active. They are growing in number—according to a conservative estimate, there are over 30 million adult evangelicals—and, even more important, they are experiencing a new vitality and a sense of self-confidence that are bringing them out of the ghetto-like existence they have led for much of the twentieth century. The rapid growth of evangelical seminaries, publishing houses, schools, magazines, and radio and television stations gives evidence of this. This new vitality and self-confidence also has a strong political dimension. Evangelical organizations with social and political agendas as diverse as Evangelicals for Social Action and the Association for Public Justice on the one hand, and the Moral Majority and Christian Voice on the other, are active and growing.

Anyone who recognizes the strength and vitality of evangelical Christianity and its renewed interest in political and social issues can see the tremendous potential evangelical Christians have for effecting political and social change in the United States. One nonevangelical student—Jeremy Rifkin, co-author with Ted Howard of *The Emerging Order* (Putnam, 1979)—has concluded, "Of one thing there is little doubt, the evangelical community is amassing a base of potential power that dwarfs every other competing interest in American society today" (p. 105). The potential is there. Let no one doubt that.

PITFALLS OF EVANGELICAL
POLITICAL INVOLVEMENT

As evangelical Christians begin assuming a more important role in American political and social life, three particularly clear pitfalls threaten them. Unless some very careful, self-conscious thinking is done, evangelicals may end up finding their best-intended efforts misdirected and ineffectual. This book is essentially an effort to understand and respond to these three pitfalls. It thereby seeks to guide those who, out of a sense of Christian love and concern, wish to play an active role in finding answers to American society's social and political problems.

The first pitfall is that for a variety of reasons, despite a resurgence of Christian interest in social and political concerns, Christians will avoid trying to make a positive impact on our society and world through direct, personal political involvement. Some fear the "dirty" reputation of politics; others are simply frightened away because to them politics is a strange world that they do not know how to go about influencing; still others are convinced the Bible teaches that it is wrong for Christians to aspire to gain and wield political power over others. The latter, who usually come out of the pacifist Anabaptist tradition, believe that Christ calls Christians to be suffering servants who turn the other cheek, not power-seeking politicians.

For one or more of these reasons, even many Christians who are socially concerned shun direct political involvement and try to influence society by means that they are more comfortable with or that they believe to be more biblical or more effective. For direct political involvement they typically substitute personal acts of love and charity, involvement in private organizations dedicated to charity and self-help projects, or attempts to live lives of radical obedience to Jesus Christ, lives that—singly or in community—can offer alternatives to the materialism, sexism, racism, and militarism of our society. Such efforts are surely not bad. They are, in fact, desperately needed in our hurting world, and God continues to bless them.

But if Christians limit their efforts to ones like these and avoid direct political involvements, they will needlessly limit the good they can do in society. God does not call all Christians—

6

nor even most Christians—to be directly and actively involved in the political processes of the nation. But I am equally convinced that he calls some Christians to undertake this task. Chapter Two makes a detailed case for certain Christians becoming personally involved in politics.

The second pitfall that evangelical Christians face is that their political impact may be bound by their sociology. Evangelicals may end up being conformed to this world by merely reflecting the dominant cultural values and perspectives of the regional, racial, economic, and social-class groups out of which they come. The danger is that the message and the impact they bring to political issues will not be controlled or shaped by the teachings of the Savior whose name they claim, but instead will be more of a reflection of their sociological background. This means that the message evangelicals would bring to the nation's political debates and struggles would not really be a Christian message at all but merely a reflection of existing political divisions in our society, now dressed up—and perhaps made even more bitter—by Christian trappings.

While I don't presume, in this small book, to outline a complete political program based on Christian principles, in Chapter Three I do suggest the starting point for looking at concrete, specific issues from a Christian perspective that promotes justice. I try to answer the question of what the goals and direction of a politically involved Christian will be.

The third danger facing evangelicals is that those who do respond to God's call to direct political involvement will waste many of their efforts because they don't completely understand politics. Their expectations may be unrealistic, their tactics inappropriate, and their accomplishments negligible. When this is the case, chances are that Christian political involvement will become erratic. Enthusiasm will periodically build up, but it will be quickly replaced by disillusionment, cynicism, and withdrawal once initial efforts are rebuffed. Or an improper accommodation to "politics as usual" may replace an original firm commitment to a biblical politics of transformation. Chapter Four considers the nature of the real political world and the ways in which it affects the Christian's attempts to use direct political involvement to promote justice and righteousness. In this chaper I try to show how such involvement must include changing the nature of the political process itself.

Finally, Chapter Five points out some practical ways concerned Christians can influence the political world by considering a variety of steps and forms of political involvement.

Earlier in this chapter I said that political involvement was a tough, sweaty business. The pitfalls to effective Christian political involvement are serious and real. In addition, the results of one's efforts are often not immediately apparent. Change comes slowly when it comes at all. But I am equally convinced that the person whom the Lord calls to be active in politics is called to serve God and humankind in a glorious, vitally important way. The issues at stake are vital, the need for justice great, and the dedicated Christian workers few. I know of no higher calling.

2

THE CASE FOR
CHRISTIAN POLITICS

I like to tell an altered version of Jesus' parable of the good Samaritan.* In this version the good Samaritan, while going down the Jerusalem-to-Jericho road a few days after finding and caring for the beaten and bruised victim of the thieves, found another victim who had been beaten and robbed. The Samaritan again showed love and concern: he poured oil on the victim's wounds, put him on his donkey and took him to an inn, and paid the innkeeper to care for the man. A week later he was taking the same trip and came upon yet another victim of thieves. Again he cared for him and took him to the inn. By now the good Samaritan was perplexed. He had made the trip from Jerusalem to Jericho many times, and until recently he had never found robbery victims on the road he traveled. So he began making inquiries around Jericho. He soon found out that the Roman governor had put a new centurion in charge of security along the Jerusalem-to-Jericho road. Many suspected he was receiving kickbacks from the thieves and that in turn he was no longer regularly patrolling the road.

The good Samaritan pondered what to do. Maybe he could make the trip to Jericho more often to look for additional victims, or maybe he could organize some of his friends and neighbors to patrol the road every day and to provide any vic-

---

*I first heard a similar version of this parable told by Lewis B. Smedes of Fuller Seminary many years ago.

tims they discovered with loving, soothing care. But he rejected these possibilities in favor of an idea that attacked the heart of the problem instead of dealing only with the symptoms. He organized a large protest rally and march, whose participants confronted the Roman governor with the problem and demanded that the corrupt centurion be replaced with someone who would restore security. The governor, fearing that stories of popular unrest would get back to Rome and reflect badly on his ability to govern, quietly removed the dishonest centurion and replaced him with one committed to maintaining safety along the Jerusalem-to-Jericho road. The rash of robberies and beatings soon diminished.

STRUCTURAL EVIL

The nature of structural evil.   The revised parable of the good Samaritan illustrates how at the root of injustices and problems in our world one sometimes finds structural evil, evil rooted in society's prevailing social, economic, or political conditions. There is a pattern to the evil because it is caused by certain social, economic, or political structures or systems. The evil the good Samaritan encountered was not merely random, nor was it caused simply by the individual actions of the thieves; it had a pattern rooted in the political system.

The pattern underlying a structural evil may be formed by certain attitudes or beliefs, as is the case with racism. When this is the case, the evil becomes part of the society's culture, supported by deeply ingrained beliefs and taboos. Or the pattern may be economic in nature. In this case the evil flows from the lack of certain economic opportunities or alternatives, a lack that forces people into poverty or unwanted occupations despite their desires, abilities, and efforts. Or the pattern may be political in nature, with the evil flowing from unjust laws or unjust law-enforcement systems. Bias and capriciousness rule, resulting in the loss of freedom and opportunity. Often structural evils are cultural, economic, and political all at once, with society's values and biases and its economic and political systems all working together to hold down a certain region or group.

Contrasting with structural evil are two other types of evil. The first is random evil, the kind typified by natural disasters or disease. A tornado can strike and destroy a family's home and possessions, or cancer can strike and render people totally incapable of helping themselves. These are evils—real, dark, and threatening—but they are seemingly random or capricious, and not caused by any societal pattern, structure, or system.

The second nonstructural evil is that arising from individual weaknesses or sins, from habits of sloth or the selfishness of putting one's self and one's immediate pleasures ahead of meeting one's obligations to others. The family that is physically terrorized and left economically destitute by a drunken parent faces an evil hatched in the dark depths of hell—but this is not structural evil. It is individual.

But if a person's cancer is caused by a chemical company's improper disposal of industrial wastes, or if a parent's drinking problem is brought on by unbearable, oppressive social and economic conditions, it takes on the coloration of structural evil. Then it is no longer truly random or simply individual; it has a causative pattern rooted in society and its cultural, economic, or political structures.

There are two crucial points to remember in all this. The first is that many of the evils present in society are structural in nature. In case after case people are trapped in prisons of oppression and fear, not because of their own actions or random catastrophies, but because of oppressive, unjust societal structures.

The second crucial point to remember is that Christians, who have been called by Jesus Christ to be a healing, comforting force in this world, must seek to move beyond merely dealing with the symptoms of oppressive structural evils. Surely Christians are called to minister to the hurting victims of the evil powers loose on this earth. But they must also be sensitive to opportunities to do more than merely give aid to the victims of structural evils; they must attack the evils themselves so that many people never become victims in the first place. If Christians do not do this, they—as a part of the society and structures that are causing the evils—are in danger of contributing to the very social, economic, or political patterns that are creating additional victims at the same time that they, through acts of Christian love and mercy, are attempting to heal the hurts of these victims! As integral members of society, Christians are often contributing to society's structural evils if they are not fighting against them.

God's answer to structural evil. Has God left his world defenseless in the face of structural evil—in the face of unjust land-ownership patterns, racism, abortion, oppressive economic systems, organized crime, and a runaway arms race? No, he has not.

There is the power of a life—or many lives—lived in the strength of Jesus Christ and in submission to God's will that can challenge and change many of today's structural evils. Jesus Christ himself, while living a life of obedience, teaching, and healing, was perceived as such a threat to the established authorities of his day that they conspired to put him to death. Unjust economic systems, racism, sexism, unjust social systems, and other evils can and have been changed by Christian lives of obedience and love.

But God has also given us government with which to fight pervasive, tenacious structural evils that hold many in the bondage of oppression and injustice. Government possesses authority and sanctions that are society-wide in their reach. This single sentence says much. Government is able to make binding decisions for all other institutions, groups, and structures in society. It can also back up its decisions with force—with the police officer's gun, the prison cell, and the fine. Thus government alone among societal institutions has the potential to make mandatory rulings that overturn evil structures and replace their evil with righteousness and justice.

As I will soon explain in detail, the heart of my case for Christian political involvement rests upon the biblical witness that this is precisely the role God intends government to play in society. And thus he calls Christian men and women to play leading roles in guiding government to fulfill its God-given destiny.

But a puzzle, a problem, immediately emerges. This problem has led many Christians to avoid direct political involvement and has contributed significantly to government's frequent failures to perform its God-given role in society. If we are to be clear on why Christians should be directly and personally involved in government as legislators, executives, judges, and interest-group leaders, we had best be clear on why so many Christians shy away from such involvement.

The puzzle is that the ethical teachings of the New Testament and the biblical injunctions concerning the divine establishment of governments and rulers seem contradictory to many. The ethical teachings of the New Testament—and of Jesus Christ in particular—are replete with references to servanthood and to eschewing force and violence, even at the risk of suffering injustices; government and law by their very nature involve authority, force, and the threat of force.

Christ's ethic of nonviolence and the suffering of injustices is clearly seen in the Sermon on the Mount:

> "You have heard that it was said, 'Eye for eye, and tooth for tooth.' But I tell you, Do not resist an evil person. If someone strikes you on the right cheek, turn to him the other also. And if someone wants to sue you and take your tunic, let him have your cloak as well. If someone forces you to go one mile, go with him two miles. Give to the one who asks you, and do not turn away from the one who wants to borrow from you." (Matt. 5:38–42)

Down through the centuries God's people have taken these visions of what it means to be Christian into a hurting, bleeding world. Thousands—even millions—of God's saints have labored as true servants of others, sacrificing fame and money, giving away possessions others hold dear, willing to give even their own lives. All this they have done in Christ's name and at his command. Saint Francis of Assisi, who gave away all his possessions to minister to the sick and poor, and Mother Theresa, who today ministers to the dying of Calcutta, are often thought to epitomize Christian servanthood. They and many like them have willingly followed in the path of Jesus, the suffering servant.

In apparent contrast to the suffering servant who gives of his or her possessions and who perhaps even gives up life itself to serve others, there is the judge, legislator, or other government official who is skilled in the development and use of political power. These individuals are part of the political system and the authority and force which belong to government.

Here indeed lies the puzzle or tension: how can Christians—whose Lord has told them to turn the other cheek and to give even to those who wrong them—participate in a system that uses the fine, the prison cell, and the gun to enforce its will? Christians are called to be servants; how can they then aspire to be judges, legislators, and police officers who wield power over others?

Many Christians, for example, are involved in health care, working as nurses, doctors, aides, and administrators in order to serve the sick and suffering of this world. To bring healing and comfort in Christ's name to those who are sick, afraid, and in pain is a deep and meaningful form of Christian service—and one with which all Christians readily and naturally identify.

But many Christians identify much less readily and naturally with the Christian public official who is struggling to hold down health-care costs in order to assure that high-quality health care will be available to all. Both in Washington, D.C., and in state capitals throughout the nation, political battles are raging over how to hold down health-care costs, which continue to rise faster than the rate of inflation. They threaten to bankrupt the Medicare program of health care for the elderly, and are putting proper health-care beyond the reach of many poor families.

The Michigan legislature has also experienced many fierce battles between the health-care providers—especially the state hospital association—and various groups both in and out of state government working to contain rising health-care costs. The problem is acute in Michigan, with the Detroit area having some of the highest medical costs in the entire nation. The state's Medicaid costs are staggering, private employers are burdened with extremely high medical-insurance costs for their employees, and low-income families without medical insurance are going without adequate medical care. On the other hand, some high-cost hospitals are facing the prospect of closing whole wings and laying off employees. Other hospitals may have to shut down entirely. As a result, bitter fights have ensued in the legislature and in executive-branch offices. Strategic moves, threats, flattery, and political pressures have been used by both sides in their struggles to bend public policy in their direction.

Many Christians are not comfortable working in such an arena. To them it seems unnatural for Christians who believe in the ethic of servanthood to seek and seize political power in order to force their view of justice and righteousness onto others. The whole business seems a bit sordid. Most Christians, given their background and training, tend to be much more comfortable ministering directly to the poor and sick as nurses, doctors, or social workers than using political power to effect needed changes in society's medical structures.

But these sorts of feelings ought not to govern Christians—or at least ought not to govern the actions or fields of service of all Christians. Surely some Christians should minister directly to the health needs of the poor and sick, but some ought also to wrestle with those structures that systematically threaten to deny good health-care to those who need it. The reason most Christians tend to respond more warmly and less ambivalently to the former than to the latter is that the church has not given adequate thought and emphasis to the God-created role of government in society and the Christian's responsibility to serve in that role.

More specifically, we as Christians need to consider two crucial elements, and when we do the tension—one might even say the contradiction—between the Christian ideal of servanthood and the proper exercise of political power disappears. What we must examine more closely are the nature of governmental authority and the ways in which God intends that authority to be exercised. In the process we will learn much about the nature of government and the Christian calling to political service.

GOVERNMENTAL AUTHORITY

The God-given authority of government. It is first of all helpful to note that the Bible teaches that government has been established by God and that people possessing governmental authority have been given that authority by God.

Moses was clearly called by God to lead Israel. Moses in turn appointed "capable men from all Israel and made them leaders of the people, officials over thousands, hundreds, fifties and tens. They served as judges for the people at all times" (Exod. 18:25–26). He later instructed the Israelites, just before they entered Canaan to take possession of it, to appoint judges and officials in every town they were to establish.

Joshua, Othniel, Gideon, Samuel, and others of the judges were specifically called by God to serve as deliverers and judges. The kings of Israel and Judah are time and again referred to as "the Lord's anointed," and in many other ways it is made clear that they held their positions and ruled with an authority given by God. For example, when both Saul and Solomon sinned against God, it was God, through his prophets, who determined and announced that their sons were to lose the kingship. When, because of the sins of Ahab and Jezebel, God decided to remove the kingship from their family, Elisha on God's instructions sent one of the prophets to anoint Jehu, the army commander, as the king in place of Joran, the son of Ahab and Jezebel: "This is what the Lord says: 'I anoint you king over Israel' " (2 Kgs. 9:3; see 2 Kgs. 9:1–29 for the story of this military coup).

The New Testament makes it clear that this divine authority of rulers was not limited to rulers of Israel, God's chosen people. When Christ was before the Roman governor Pilate and refused to answer some of his questions, Pilate asked, "Do you refuse to speak to me? Don't you realize I have power either to free you or to crucify you?" Jesus replied, "You would have no power over me if it were not given you from above" (John 19:10–11). Romans 13 very explicitly declares, "Everyone must submit himself to the governing authorities, for there is no authority except that which God has established. The authorities that exist have been established by God. Consequently, he who rebels against the authority is rebelling against what God has instituted . . ." (vv. 1–2).

The witness of the Bible is clear: government is part of God's will for regulating the affairs of human society, and those who rule therefore do so under his authority.

The nature of governmental authority.   If we are to understand the God-intended role of governmental authority in human society and how it fits in with the ethic of the Sermon on the Mount, it is important that we look more closely at the nature of the governmental authority God has established.

As noted earlier, governments are characterized by the use of force and the threat of force. But the exercise of force is not the same as the exercise of authority. Governments do not simply exercise force or coercion; they exercise authority backed by force or coercion. Force or coercion is limited and channeled by the authority government possesses—and that makes all the difference.

Perhaps a story that I first used in my earlier book, *The Unraveling of America*, will help. Once there were two men, both of whom suffered misfortunes one evening. The first man decided that since it was a delightfully cool April evening he would go for a stroll in a nearby park before retiring for the evening. But while he was walking, a thief leaped out from some bushes, held a gun against his back, and demanded his money. Unfortunately, our victim had just cashed a check and was carrying a hundred dollars in his wallet. The thief quickly took the money and made his escape before any help could arrive. Our victim went home a poorer man.

That same evening, the other man was struggling with his annual income-tax forms. He figured and refigured columns of numbers, but each time he came to the same conclusion: he owed the government an additional one hundred dollars in taxes. Finally giving up in disgust, he reached for his checkbook, wrote out a hundred-dollar check, stuffed it and the appropriate forms into an envelope, and mailed them off to the Internal Revenue Service. He too went to bed that evening a poorer man.

Superficially, these two men suffered similar fates: both gave up a hundred dollars they wanted to keep, and both acted under coercion or the threat of sanctions (the gun and physical harm in one case, and fines and possible imprisonment in the other). Both the gunman and the government possessed power over their respective victims; both were able to force their victims to do things they preferred not to do.

But here the similarity ends. The man who lost his money to the thief never for a moment would imagine that the thief had a right to demand the money and that he had an obligation to give it. It was a matter of physical coercion, pure and simple.

In the case of the tax-paying citizen, he probably would acknowledge, even while wishing he could keep the money, that the government had the right to demand taxes and that he had an obligation to pay them. In other words, the government, unlike the thief, possessed authority—that is, the rightful ability to command the obedience of another individual in a particular situation in order to achieve a particular goal or result.

Parents exercise authority over their children, employers over employees, teachers over students, elders or bishops over the church, and government over citizens. In all these cases authority is backed up by penalties: the parent may spank a child, an employer may fire an employee, a teacher may fail a student, the church may excommunicate a member, and government may imprison a citizen. But this force is not at the heart of the nature of authority. What is at its heart is the rightness or moral appropriateness of one person commanding another.

But what is the source of this morally appropriate action? The Bible frequently teaches that the moral rightness of one person's commanding the obedience of another under certain circumstances—that is, authority—is part of God's will for human society.

The Bible is filled with references to relationships of authority that are approved by God and are part of his order for human society. Parental authority is affirmed and given divine blessing by commands such as "Children, obey your parents in the Lord, for this is right" (Eph. 6:1). Biblical teachings concerning the master-slave relationship are relevant to today's authority relationship between employer and employee—for example, "Slaves, obey your earthly masters in everything; and do it, not only when their eye is on you and to win their favor, but with sincerity of heart and reverence for the Lord" (Col. 3:22). Peter compares an elder's relationship to the members of his church with a shepherd's relationship to his sheep, and refers to them as overseers; Paul makes it clear that a bishop or overseer "is entrusted with God's work" (Titus 1:7). In all these relationships—parent to child, supervisor to worker, church officeholder to church member—authority is present. One person commands the obedience of another, and the ability to do so is rooted in God's will for humankind.

Yet authority by its very nature is limited. Authority is the rightful ability to command obedience of another *in a particular situation and for a particular purpose*. Authority always has limits, points at which it ceases to be applicable. Parents may rightfully command their child to eat a balanced diet, but they have no right to command their child to do something life-threatening—and no right to command a neighbor's child at all. Parents' authority is limited both to commands involving their own children and to actions that are designed to achieve the purposes for which they were given authority. Their exercise of force or sanctions is thereby also circumscribed, since they may exercise force only in support of this limited authority. The authority of employers or church officials is similarly circumscribed. It applies only to those people under supervision, and only to very limited areas of their lives.

This is the type of authority that the Bible has in mind when it refers to the authority of those who govern in the political world. They exercise a real, divinely given authority that is backed up by coercive sanctions but that is also limited.

Various biblical passages command the Christian not to resort to force but to give even to those who demand unjustly. But these passages clearly cannot refer to those people properly exercising the authority given to them. Surely Christ would not want parents to interpret his command to "give to the one who asks you" to mean they should comply if their children ask not to be disciplined. In the same way God has given Christian judges the authority to rule with justice, and thus God hardly expects them not to "resist an evil person" in the exercise of their official duties. A Christian judge whose wife has been murdered would be required *as a husband* to forgive and show kindness to the murderer, but also *as a judge*—if one can imagine the accused murderer coming before his bench—to mete out punishment to the same person.

In summary, the tension between the two pictures mentioned earlier—that of the humble, self-denying Christian of the Sermon on the Mount and that of the public official wielding power over others—is caused in part by the false assumption that physical coercion and political authority are the same. They are not. Physical coercion in the form of naked force is condemned by God, and is to be rejected. Political authority—and the coercion that backs it up—is divinely given. Its appropriate use thereby has God's blessing.

THE EXERCISE OF GOVERNMENTAL AUTHORITY

All authority given by God is given for a certain purpose—a purpose that channels and directs the use of that authority. This raises the question of the purpose of God-given governmental authority. This is a crucial question because it is this purpose that—by channeling and directing that authority—puts additional constraints upon it and helps to explain further the compatibility of the exercise of political power with the ethic of the Sermon on the Mount.

Justice: the purpose of government's authority. God has established rulers on earth in order to promote justice and to fight oppression, evil, and injustice. Moses clearly was speaking God's will when he gave these instructions to the rulers and judges the Israelites were to appoint in the towns they were to establish in the promised land: "They shall judge the people fairly. Do not pervert justice or show partiality. Do not accept a bribe, for a bribe blinds the eyes of the wise and twists the words of the righteous. Follow justice and justice alone . . ." (Deut. 16:18–20).

The Old Testament prophets repeatedly had to condemn the kings and other rulers of Israel for their failure to uphold a just legal system. Isaiah declared:

> Woe to those who make unjust laws,
>   to those who issue oppressive decrees,
> to deprive the poor of their rights
>   and rob my oppressed people of justice,
> making widows their prey
>   and robbing the fatherless. (10:1–2)

Ezekiel wrote: "This is what the Sovereign Lord says: 'You have gone far enough, O princes of Israel! Give up your violence and oppression and do what is just and right. Stop dispossessing my people,' declares the Sovereign Lord" (45:9).

Amos condemned those who "oppress the righteous and take bribes and . . . deprive the poor of justice in the courts" (5:12). And Habakkuk complained to God:

Why do you make me look at injustice?
Why do you tolerate wrong?
Destruction and violence are before me;
there is strife, and conflict abounds.
Therefore the law is paralyzed,
and justice never prevails.
The wicked hem in the righteous,
so that justice is perverted. (1:3–4)

In Psalm 72 the poet paints a picture of the righteous ruler:

Endow the king with your justice, O God,
the royal son with your righteousness.
He will judge your people in righteousness,
your afflicted ones with justice. . . .
He will defend the afflicted among the people
and save the children of the needy;
he will crush the oppressor. (vv. 1–2,4)

Clearly God intended the rulers of Israel to execute justice, to prevent corruption, and to protect the poor and weak in society from being exploited by the evil and the powerful.

The New Testament testifies that this role of government in the Old Testament nation of Israel has an application broader than that of the Israelites. Romans 13 is particularly clear on this point. It teaches not only that rulers are granted their authority by God but also that their authority is to be used to promote good and to restrain evil:

For rulers hold no terror for those who do right, but for those who do wrong. Do you want to be free from fear of the one in authority? Then do what is right and he will commend you. For he is God's servant to do you good. But if you do wrong, be afraid, for he does not bear the word for nothing. He is God's servant, an agent of wrath to bring punishment on the wrongdoer. (vv. 3–4)

The language of this passage is strong and explicit. Rulers are God's servants. They serve God by rewarding good and punishing evil. Similarly, Peter writes of governors being established by God "to punish those who do wrong and to commend those who do right" (1 Pet. 2:14).

The conclusion is clear: God has established government as his means to work in society for justice and righteousness and against oppression and evil. Since government is the only institution with both society-wide authority and the "power of the sword"—means by which to enforce its authority—it is often the only means, and surely the most direct means, with which to attack the culturally embedded attitudes and the oppressive evils that lie at the heart of pervasive structural evils. And that is precisely what God calls government to do, that is precisely why he has established and given governmental authority to those who rule.

Thus those who rule wisely and well are acting as God's servants. Their calling is holy; they are doing God's work on earth. This means that those who rule—judges, prosecutors, legislators, chief executives, and a host of other government officials—are following a divine calling and that Christians who are called to serve God in government ought not to resist that call. They are being called to be God's servants. This is also true of those who involve themselves in politics by supporting those who are seeking public office or who in other ways are trying to influence the course of political events.

The danger of perverted government. There is, however, a problem. The more powerful persons or institutions can be for good, the more powerful they can also be for evil. The wise, energetic person can do more good—and more evil—than a lazy fool. Similarly, government—that institution God has equipped to be a powerful means to redress wrongs and establish justice— has a tremendous potential for evil. Human society already has a tendency to produce evil structures in which the powerful oppress the poor and vulnerable, and government is meant to fight such structures. But government itself can all too easily become an evil structure, beholden to and responsive to the already powerful in society who then greatly increase their economic and social power by adding political power to it.

A little reflection will tell one why this is in fact a common pattern in the political world. When one says "politics" one says "power." Whether one is talking about an election campaign or the internal politics of a legislature or other governmental institution, one is talking about people pursuing power. The possession of power can mean many things—and most of them appeal to our selfish natures. Above all it means being deferred to and being surrounded by a hundred little reminders every day that you are someone, that you are important. It means a staff that serves you at your command; it means lobbyists who will entertain and flatter you; it means people who are delighted just to get an appointment with you; it means people standing up and applauding when you are introduced—or when you simply walk into a room; it means having your name in the headlines and appearing on television and radio; it means being recognized as a person of standing and importance in your community. It means all this and more. To take an ordinary human being whose nature is already marred by a sinful inclination to put self above all, and to say, "All this is yours if only you will, bit by bit and day by day, take care of others only after the needs of your own ambitions have been met"—to do so is to confront many people with a temptation that is too strong for them to resist. It is those who are already powerful in society—those with money, position, prestige, and influence—who can often turn government to their own selfish purposes by offering those in political office what seems necessary to fulfill their own ambitions.

Government then becomes blasphemous, because it comes to serve the cause of evil instead of good, injustice instead of justice. Instead of being the servants of God, rulers then become servants of the dark forces of evil. Therefore, God's gift to humankind, which he meant to be a tool to limit the effects of sin and enable all his children to live in peace and justice, is in constant peril of being subverted by the evil against which it is supposed to be struggling.

Thus it becomes essential, if we are not to lose this God-given means of establishing his will on earth, that Christians do all they can to maintain government as a caring, justice-defending structure. Constant vigilance and constant involvement are essential if God's means of promoting justice is not to be turned into a means of reinforcing injustice. Christians have the sense of purpose and mission necessary to resist the seduction of power and prestige that can cause many to fall and—collectively—to turn government away from its God-given purposes in a sinful world.

The servant-politician. If government's God-given purposes are in fact not to be subverted, those with governmental authority must understand the way in which God intends their authority to be exercised. It is easy to assume that those in positions of political authority are the ones in charge—the ones calling the shots—and that those who are subject to their authority are the servants, the ones who meekly obey when commanded. After all, authority implies issuing commands, being in charge, being important. Being a servant implies the opposite: obeying commands, being subservient, being of little importance.

But this assumption is false. Paradoxically, the exact opposite is true in God's ordering of the world. Those in authority should always exercise their authority so as to become servants of those they oversee. This is crucial.

Several years ago in Jackson, Michigan, the football coach of a Catholic high school was brutally murdered. He was a very successful and well-liked coach whose team had won the state football championship the previous year. At his funeral the Reverend Father Joseph Coyle, the president of the school, said this: "Jim Crowly wasn't just a coach. Jim was a servant of each and every boy he coached."

At first these words sound strange. How could a tough football coach be a servant of his players? A man who can expell any player from the team for breaking a team rule? who shuffles players from one position to another, perhaps against their will? A sports coach appears to be more of a dictator than a servant.

But coaches should always exercise their authority so as to become servants of their players. A coach's authority is to be used not to meet his or her own ego needs but to benefit the players and the team. Good coaches will even deny many of their own needs and desires in order to spend more time with players who need additional help or attention, or will build up the team's confidence by taking less of the credit due them and giving more credit to the players. In the process the coach in a very real sense becomes a servant of the players. It is—or at least should be—the same for all authority relationships. Peter makes a similar point in discussing the authority of church elders: "Be shepherds of God's flock that is under your care, serving as overseers—not because you must, but because you are willing, as God wants you to be; not greedy for money, but eager to serve; not lording

24

it over those entrusted to you, but being examples to the flock"
(1 Pet. 5:2–3).

Similarly, the Christ-like ideal for the public official is that
of the servant-politician. The servant-politician is the legislator,
bureaucrat, judge, or other government official who possesses
political authority. By enacting or enforcing laws or by passing
judgment, he or she can rightfully command obedience from
others. But this authority is used in God's service in such a way
that the person possessing it becomes a servant of those whom
he or she governs. Authority—and the power that goes with it—is
not to be used for self-aggrandizement or financial gain, or to
achieve success or command the deference others may show. All
this must count as "loss compared to the surpassing greatness of
knowing Christ Jesus my Lord, for whose sake I have lost all
things. I consider them rubbish, that I may gain Christ . . ."
(Phil. 3:8). Servant-politicians lose all that the world considers
important so that they may use their power to serve others. They
become "God's servants" by serving all of God's children.

Honor, acclaim, and fame may or may not come. Whether
or not they do is irrelevant. Exercising political authority as a
faithful servant of the public is what God calls the servant-
politician to do; whether doing so faithfully leads to acclaim and
higher office or to anonymity and a shortened political career
is for God to decide. Just as coaches subjugate their needs and
desires to those of their players and parents subjugate their needs
and desires to those of their children, so servant-politicians subjugate their needs and desires to those of the public.

Thus the servant-legislator will pursue a cause that is just,
spending precious time and effort doing so even though no one
may notice and no acclaim may follow. It may even result in
criticism and the loss of votes in the next election. But he or she
persists because there are people in need and he or she is their
servant.

The servant-judge or the servant-bureaucrat acts in the same
way as the servant-legislator. The servant-judge will be helpful
to the frightened, confused witness, will be patient with an
overbearing attorney, and will take pains to give a fair trial to
an apparently guilty defendant even when the community is calling for a quick trial and harsh punishment. He or she does all

this because—even while exercising immense authority—he or she is a servant of the witnesses, attorneys, and defendants appearing before the bench.

The servant-bureaucrat will apply the law fairly and equally, whether dealing with a large, powerful corporation that has friends in high places or with a small, weak business that has few friends in the capital. In interpreting the law, the servant-bureaucrat will be guided by fairness, equity, and need, not by what is the best career move.

The servant-legislator who risks electoral defeat by voting for a measure that is as unpopular as it is necessary to protect some of God's weak children, the servant-judge who insists on a fair trial for an arrogant, obnoxious defendant, the servant-bureaucrat who is fair to the powerful and the powerless alike—all are turning the other cheek and going the second mile. They are living according to the stirring and challenging ethics of the Sermon on the Mount, which puts others and their welfare before self and its desires. Paradoxically, power and servanthood do mix as long as power is exercised in service to God.

In summary, my case for Christians' direct involvement in politics is this: government has been established by God as a key means to pursue justice and to oppose unjust, oppressive structures in society. Even when it becomes necessary for a Christian public official to use force to back up his or her authority, such actions have God's blessing as long as the authority is being exercised properly. There is a constant danger that government will be subverted and turned away from its justice-promoting role. This makes the need for Christian involvement in government even more urgent. By getting involved in politics, Christians make themselves servants of others, working for the good of others before seeking their own ease, convenience, and security.

THE POLITICAL COMPONENT
OF TODAY'S CRUCIAL ISSUES

The core of the case for Christian political involvement lies in what has already been presented. But a final important point is this: the most crucial social issues or problems facing the United

States and the world today have very strong political dimensions, dimensions that, if ignored, will greatly limit one's ability to positively affect those issues. This means that if the church—not the institutional church but Christ's body of believers here on earth—is to be an effective servant to the world's hurting multitudes, it simply must be deeply involved in politics in a direct, persistent way.

I would challenge everyone to make up a list of the·five most crucial issues or problems facing American society and the world in the last two decades of the twentieth century—the five societal problems that will most deeply affect people and their ability to live free, God-honoring, joyful lives. The lists would differ widely, but whatever their specific contents, most if not all of the items noted would be issues that have very significant political components.

My own list would include, first of all, the continuing and very real possibility of nuclear holocaust. The full horror of the current stockpiles of thousands of nuclear weapons is beyond comprehension. God holds every single human life in the highest esteem—every person is precious, created in the image of God himself. Yet humankind has created and presumably is prepared to use weapons that would indiscriminately kill hundreds of millions of precious men, women, and children in a few minutes. Surely Christians must do all they can to pull humankind back from this awful precipice.

This means politics. It is governments that have created nuclear weapons and the ways to deploy them. It is government leaders who would make the fateful decision to unleash the ultimate horror of nuclear war on this planet. Thus one must be politically involved to influence policies on nuclear armament. There can be no higher service to all God's children on this earth than preventing the use of nuclear weapons.

A second issue I would include on my list is the need for a stable economy, one that offers people opportunities to provide for themselves and their families through useful employment, and spares them the pain of disruptions such as rapid, destructive inflation. It is right and good for people to want to work—to contribute to society by helping to provide goods or services and thereby to support themselves and their families.

For such people to be told that there is no useful work for them to do, that there is no way for them to earn a living, is dehumanizing and destructive of what God intends for all his children. Rapid inflation has a similar, if less dramatic, effect: it can undo the responsible actions of individuals who want to be self-supporting. To be able to be the free, contributing, creative, and responsible individuals God intends them to be, people must be able to find safe, decent employment and be spared the destructive results of high inflation or other severe economic disruptions.

In today's world it is clear that when one says "economic issues" one says "government." Governments' involvement in economics is deep and pervasive. Inflation or stability, recession and depression or economic growth are direct consequences of public-policy decisions. Certainly there is room for economic self-help projects and for private job-training and employment programs. But these are all carried on within a context of more general economic trends and conditions that can help or hinder such efforts—and these trends and conditions are largely the consequence, for good or ill, of government policies. Therefore, one crucial way to be a servant to the poor and the unemployed is to work politically for policies that will help assure a stable economy with ample jobs. Without the proper economic policies the positive results of all the best efforts at self-help and private employment and training will be canceled out.

The third major issue I would put on my list of crucial issues is the problem of desperate poverty found in many so-called third-world nations—those nations outside the liberal democracies of North America and Western Europe, the authoritarian regime of the Soviet Union, and the communist nations of Eastern Europe and Asia. In many nations of South America, Africa, and Asia, hunger, poverty, and disease are constant realities. Life is too often short and devoid of the opportunities and joys that should inhere in being an image-bearer of God Almighty. Especially with Christ's church growing rapidly in many areas of the third world, increasing numbers of North American Christians are quite properly becoming more concerned with the plight of their Christian brothers and sisters in the southern half of the world. Church relief-agencies that distribute food, teach appropriate agricultural techniques, and bring modern medicine stand as present-day fulfillments of Christ's command to care for the needy and to heal the sick.

Yet one is soon forced to recognize that unless Christians try to deal with the political aspects of this situation, the church will be reduced largely to dealing with symptoms. We will be like the good Samaritan who keeps on taking beaten travelers to the inn but never tries to get rid of the corrupt centurion. Very basic causes of the desperate poverty of the third world are the political and economic policies of powerful Western nations, including the United States. Our government has opposed and worked against reformist governments that would have reduced the profits of American corporations but also would have improved the lot of their people by such steps as land reform. The poorest country in the western hemisphere is probably Haiti. Hundreds—perhaps thousands—die each year from hunger and malnutrition. Yet in 1980 the United States imported $30 million of food from Haiti! Trade policies of the United States often work to the disadvantage of the poor countries. One must be careful not to oversimplify an admittedly complex situation, and certainly the United States and other Western nations are not the only—and often not even the major—cause of poverty in third-world nations. Yet American policies and the actions of American corporations all too often hinder rather than encourage desperately needed reforms. As a result, caring about the poor and hungry of the world necessarily means a large measure of political involvement.

The fourth major issue I would put on my list is how American society will react to the growing scarcity of fossil fuels and other natural resources vital to American industry and the American standard of living. Within the lifetimes of the majority of today's Americans the structure of our society will undergo major changes because of the increasing scarcity, and therefore the sharply increased costs, of fossil fuels—especially oil and gas—and certain important minerals. As a consequence, American society could face an increasing disparity between the rich and poor, with more and more of the middle class slipping into poverty. Revolution and major social disruptions would become ever more likely. On the other hand, society could be marked by a greater sharing of available resources and an acceptance of certain restraints in order to make available resources go farther. I am confident that it is not God's will that a very small elite enjoy lives of extreme luxury while many are barely able to stay alive or at best live dreary lives devoid of opportunities to experience the joys of education, travel, the arts, and recreation.

It is clear that the society-wide nature of the problem will result in government's playing a key role in reacting to it. Public policies—whether the government's involvement in them be extensive or minimal—will be developed, and they will have a profound impact on American society and its millions of people. The conclusion is inescapable: if Christians are going to be servants of the people as they confront a developing energy problem, they must speak and act politically in regard to changing allocations of energy and other resources.

The fifth and final crucial issue I would put on my list is present-day racism and the continuing consequences of past racist policies. Because black slavery was practiced for over two hundred years in North America, American society is biracial, but it is not an equal society. American slavery, unjust laws that existed for a hundred years after slavery was abolished, and persistent prejudices have taken and continue to take their toll in terms of the lack of opportunities afforded black Americans. The results are all around us. There is too high a percentage of blacks among the poor and the low-income groups, in our nation's prisons, in the poorest schools and colleges, and in unskilled jobs. And there is too low a percentage of blacks belonging to the middle- and upper-income groups, attending the better schools and colleges, and holding skilled jobs. American society is divided and unequal. As long as this is true, we will continue to reap a bitter harvest.

Of the five issues I have listed, this is the one where the potential for good, for healing through direct, private actions by both black and white Christians, overshadows what can be done through government action. Most of the needed political actions were taken in the 1950s and 1960s, when legal barriers to a society undivided by race were struck down. Christians must work politically to guard against the reimposition of these barriers and to search for public policies that will help heal the wounds of a three-hundred-year history of rabid discrimination against black Americans. But most of the healing, I suspect, must come through countless acts of reconciliation, forgiveness, and love. Through such acts black Christians and white Christians will become servants of each other.

Other lists of the five most crucial problems facing American society and the world would differ somewhat from mine. But I am convinced that these lists—whatever the specific issues included—would involve areas in which public policies will have to play a major role in shaping their solutions. This is not an argument for big government. It is simply a recognition that in modern, interdependent societies the quality of our lives—the level of opportunities to live lives of joy and service, as God intended us to—is profoundly affected by conditions over which individuals and small groups have no control and by decisions made thousands of miles away from where they live. Thus there must be a political dimension to the commitment of Christians dedicated to following God's command to be servants to others by seeking their good.

By this—and by this entire chapter—I do not mean to imply that all Christians must immerse themselves in political action. The Bible teaches that Christ's body, the church, operates according to a division of labor. I am certain that there are many Christians whom God is not calling to be directly and deeply involved in politics. But I am equally certain of two things: first, that all Christians should at least be interested, participating citizens, and second, that God is calling certain Christians to a deeper, more active involvement in the political life of the nation.

3

THE BASIS FOR CHRISTIAN POLITICS

It was a strange sight. Hundreds of parked motorcycles circled the state capitol. Inside, hundreds of motorcyclists, with their long hair and beards, their leather jackets and boots, prowled the corridors and packed the visitors' galleries of the legislative chambers. Each one seemed to fit the stereotype of a motorcycle-gang member. Never in my eight years in the Michigan legislature had I been lobbied by a tougher-looking group of citizens, nor—paradoxically—had I ever known a group to lobby so heavily on the basis of abstract concepts of right and wrong. They passionately argued their case on the basis of justice, personal rights, freedom, and fairness.

The issue was whether or not Michigan should require motorcyclists to wear safety helmets while riding their motorcycles. The motorcyclists argued on the basis of facts: they cited studies purporting to show that helmets do not add to the safety of their wearers. They argued on the basis of justice and freedom: the state should not interfere with their freedom of choice because even if helmets do add to safety, they add to the safety not of society but of the one who wears the helmet. They argued on the basis of fairness: mandatory helmet laws are hypocritical and based on prejudice against "bikers," as they referred to themselves. After all, they pointed out, the legislature hadn't taken other comparable actions, such as banning cigarettes and requiring car passengers to wear seat belts, rulings that would have at least as clear a link to health or safety as helmet-wearing.

I had to agree that they had a point. Government ought not to be a big brother imposing on the public its judgment of what is healthy and safe. Freedom must include the freedom to do unwise things—and to live with the consequences. Justice cannot mean protecting people from their own foolishness.

On the other hand, it became clear to me as I studied the issue that helmets do improve the chances of one's surviving an accident on a motorcycle. And when a cyclist dies or is seriously and permanently injured because he wasn't wearing a helmet, all of society is affected. Insurance rates for all of us increase; surviving spouses or children may need to go on welfare; medical bills for long-term hospitalization, rehabilitation therapy, and nursing-home care are borne by all of us. Also to be weighed is the emotional agony suffered by the driver of the car that strikes and kills or seriously injures a motorcyclist—death or injury that might have been prevented by the simple expedient of the motorcyclist's wearing a helmet.

In such a situation, how does one apply the conclusion reached in Chapter Two that the God-given purpose of government is to work for justice and righteousness and against oppression and evil? Where in fact lies the justice of which Moses, Habakkuk, Amos, and others spoke in ringing words? On the side of increasing individuals' freedom of choice? Or on the side of protecting people—and, indirectly, society—from carelessness? The correct answer is not immediately clear or obvious.

It is usually—I am tempted to write "always"—so in the real political world. Issues of justice, freedom, and righteousness almost never come in grand and glorious watershed issues where the consequences for more or less justice, freedom, and righteousness are immediate and clear. Instead, issues of justice and righteousness come disguised in the form of specific, usually very narrow, often technical—and perhaps what seem to be almost inconsequential—questions.

The helmet law is one example. Another is the issue of whether the allowable level of a deadly chemical in food is to be set at three parts per million or three parts per billion. Or whether welfare recipients who fail to participate in a job-training program should be dropped from the welfare rolls for sixty days or ninety days—or perhaps for longer or shorter time periods. Or whether F-16 fighters should be sold to Israel and AWACS planes to Saudi Arabia. Or whether dairy-price supports should be set at $13.10 per hundred-weight or at some higher or lower figure. One could go on and on. The point is that political decisions are typically narrow, specific, and often technical. Justice and righteousness are thereby forged—or destroyed—by thousands of such decisions, many of which are seemingly far removed from grand philosophic discussions of biblical justice.

The situation is similar to that of a marriage, which is molded either into a joyful, God-honoring union in service to him and humankind or into a self-centered, tension-filled relationship that barely stays out of the divorce courts. Though opposite, both relationships are determined not by one or two acts or decisions but by innumerable small, often unselfconscious acts and decisions of the husband and wife. So also justice is achieved not by one or two self-conscious, earthshaking decisions but by countless small, concrete determinations usually made without thought to their wider implications for a more just social order.

This means that Christians seeking to move government toward greater justice—whether as officeholders or as citizens— face two dangers. The first is that they will miss completely the implications for justice present in the many specific, often technical issues that government deals with daily. If they are only looking out for one or two crucial, watershed issues that obviously involve considerations of justice, they will miss the multitude of narrower issues that cumulatively have a much bigger impact on the government's promotion or weakening of a just order.

We all recognize the oversight of the home owner who worries that a catastrophic fire will destroy his house and takes many precautions to prevent such a calamity, but pays no attention to the danger posed by millions of termites that, undetected and unseen, are destroying his house bit by bit. Similarly, public officials may be allowing all kinds of injustices to creep into the system even when they desire to be—and think they in fact are— on the side of justice, simply because they are not paying attention to numerous policy decisions that appear to be technical and almost inconsequential but that in fact do have implications for justice. The same thing can happen to citizens and citizen groups who are concerned with justice.

The second danger that arises from the fact that justice—or injustice—largely flows from innumerable specific, narrow decisions is that those who begin their political involvements with very high ideals of pursuing justice can, after a while, find themselves wallowing in the swamp of selfish ambition. These people would never have ended up far from the firm path of justice-guided politics if such straying had involved one or two fundamental, watershed decisions. But they became victims of selfish aspiration by taking one small, seemingly innocuous step after another. It happens so easily and naturally because it happens without one ever making a self-conscious decision to chuck one's ideals and join in the politics of self-interest and self-aggrandizement. It takes God's grace, constant vigilance, and a precise, self-conscious understanding of justice as a guiding, discerning principle to avoid having one's ideals subverted. A group as well as an individual can fall prey to this danger if it succumbs to making one small accommodation after another in an attempt to maintain or increase its stature and influence and that of its leaders.

The way to avoid both of these dangers is to do very clear, careful thinking about justice and how it lies—and often lies hidden—in the questions and decisions that government is usually dealing with. A self-conscious, discerning, biblically rooted perspective is essential.

However, as soon as we turn to the Bible to discover the principles and standards that will give us such a perspective, we realize that the Bible is no more a neat, simple handbook to the understanding of today's political issues and how the Christian should react to them than it is an easy guide to the understanding of today's scientific issues and controversies. The Old Testament was written in the context of a theistic, tribal society in which there was no separation of what we would call church and state. The New Testament was written in the context of a small, subjugated people and of a new, emerging "sect" in a world dominated by a totally autocratic military power. Thus it is not surprising that the Bible cannot function as a neat, easy reference-book in which we can look up answers to today's political issues and problems.

However, the Bible clearly does contain principles applicable to political life today, principles that are absolute and true and relevant to all times and all places. It is equally clear that our Lord expects us to use the knowledge and understanding he has given us to apply these principles to our own society and time.

We are still a long way from knowing the nature and content of the biblical principles that will help us decide whether or not to require motorcyclists to wear helmets or at what level to set dairy-price supports. We need to develop a standard that is biblically based and yet applicable to today's specific, concrete, often seemingly mundane political issues. It is to this task we now turn.

SOCIETY, ORDER, AND JUSTICE

In today's world the more general biblical calls for government to promote justice and righteousness and to oppose oppression and evil can best be seen in terms of public or political justice. The concept of justice grows naturally out of the broader biblical principles cited in the previous chapter and can serve as a reliable—although not automatic or self-applying—guide for judging and reacting to the specific issues and questions arising in contemporary American politics.

To understand the meaning of political or public justice, we should start with the fact that men and women are created by God in his image to be free, loving, creative, joyful beings, living lives of praise to God and service to others. That is humankind's God-given purpose. Unlike animals, we have been created by God to be freely choosing, morally responsible, creative beings. The entire Bible teaches this—from the account of Adam and Eve in the Garden of Eden to John's urging persons in the last chapter of Revelation to accept "the free gift of the water of life" (22:17). Christ's summary of the greatest commandment, which is to love God above all and our neighbor as ourselves (Matt. 22:37–40), also supports this conclusion.

The earth God created is incredibly beautiful, its natural resources exceedingly abundant, and men and women themselves capable of a creative joy and love that can lift the human experience far above even the natural beauties and riches of this earth. The surf breaking upon a broad expanse of beach as the sun slowly lightens the east, young parents holding their newborn child in a loving embrace, a graceful bridge spanning a broad, rushing river—these pictures evoke images of the world as God intended it to be: a place of joy, beauty, peace, and creative opportunities.

It is important to note that for human beings to be free to live lives of creative joy and love, as God intends them to, society must be marked by a just order. Three terms are crucial here: "society," "order," and "just."

First, of course, is society. Human beings have been created by God to live with each other. We are social beings: we need each other in order to develop into the thinking, choosing, communicating, loving beings God intends us to be. It is only in community with others that we can become all that God wants us to be. That much is clear.

Second, for human beings to live together, society must be marked by order. "Order" refers to a situation in which human relationships and expectations are regularized by adherence to established rules, customs, and standards. Without this, all human relationships would be based on caprice and happenstance. Chaos would be king, brute force the only law. For human society to exist at all, there must be some way to establish regularized patterns of behavior. In an orderly world there is some way to determine what type of clothing is suitable for what occasions, on which side of the road cars should be driven, and whether or not punching someone in the nose is appropriate behavior. Customs, tradition, and law all play a part in bringing about order.

My point here is that if there is no order, then there can be no society, and if there is no society, human beings cannot be the loving, joyful, creative beings God intends them to be.

The third significant component is justice. There can be a just order or an unjust order in society—the distinction is crucial. Justice has traditionally been defined as giving all persons their due. The basic idea is that all people, as created image-bearers of God, possess certain rights that are their due, that are theirs simply because they are human. The right to life itself and the right to worship God freely are examples. Of course, people often disagree on exactly what is due an individual, and thus what rights a society must respect if it is to have a just order. At the heart of the answer must lie that which is necessary or helpful in order for people to live the joyful, creative, loving lives God intends for all his children. At the very least, then, a just order will protect basic freedoms and work to assure a broad range of opportunities for all.

This means that under a just order people will not find their lives totally predetermined and controlled by outside forces. An order imposed by a totalitarian government that dictates one's occupation, restricts one's travel, denies one freedom of religion, controls the upbringing of one's children, denies one the freedom to speak or publish one's beliefs, and in numerous other ways controls one's life—such an order clearly and obviously violates justice. There is no freedom; there is no opportunity to be a freely choosing, creative, morally responsible individual. One's life is reduced to the existence of a dog or a horse that is led about by its master. To be totally controlled is to be treated as less than human. Similarly, a person living in a primitive tribal society in which one's whole life and almost every act is circumscribed by extremely rigid traditions and taboos can also be denied the creative freedom God intends for all of us, even in the absence of formally enacted laws.

Closer to home, economic conditions and societal attitudes can also help create an unjust order that denies people the basic freedom God intends for them. Take the case of a young black woman living in extreme poverty in an urban ghetto. There are no laws forbidding her to aspire to be the owner-operator of a small plant manufacturing component parts for computers. Indeed, she may be called by God to praise him and serve others by pursuing this dream. But the order existing in American society conspires to raise almost insurmountable barriers to her achieving this goal. Racism and sexism make women and blacks less than fully welcomed in the manufacturing sector of the economy and surely not welcome as owners of high-tech businesses. Coming from a background of poverty, this woman will probably not be able to get the high-quality education she would need to attain this goal. In all probability the elementary schools and high schools in her neighborhood are low-quality institutions that have profound disciplinary problems and offer little intellectual stimulation. And she may not be able to afford a college education.

My point here is that the suffocating of freedom and opportunities—that is, an unjust order—can arise from societal attitudes, traditions, and structures as well as from the more easily recognized unjust laws. Justice is not merely a negative concept, not only the absence of certain restraints on our activities; it is also a positive concept—the existence of actual opportunities that allow us to make morally responsible choices.

I have thus far introduced two key social elements: (1) humankind's God-given purpose—to live loving, joyful, creative lives of praise and service—and (2) a just order—societal customs, traditions, and laws that protect basic freedoms and assure a broad range of opportunities. These two elements are related, of course, for it is the freedoms and opportunities assured by a just order that enable men and women to fulfill their God-given purpose.

But an important point still needs to be made. Respect for the basic freedoms and opportunities that are due every individual—that is, justice—can be secured only if a society's members accept certain obligations. Your right to life is bought by my accepting my obligation not to kill you. Freedoms and opportunities are not free; their cost is the imposition of obligations on society. Working to establish a just order thus becomes the difficult task of deciding what freedoms to recognize and what opportunities to protect at the cost of imposing certain obligations. Is protecting the unborn child's right to life worth imposing on a pregnant woman the obligation to carry a fetus to term? Is my opportunity for a free college education worth imposing additional taxes on the rest of society? Is the opportunity to enjoy clean, clear streams worth imposing on both individuals and businesses the obligation not to pollute, even if that means certain manufactured goods will cost more or some people will lose their jobs? This is the appropriate way to frame every issue if a society is sincere about pursuing the goal of a just order.

It is a matter of deciding what freedoms and opportunities are worth the imposition of certain obligations. The standard to be used in making these determinations is the goal of increasing the actual free range of choices available to all God's children to live as he intended them to: in praise and service, with joy, love, and creativity. A just order thereby emerges.

But when confronted with specific, concrete political issues, how does one determine the balance between freedoms or opportunities on the one hand and obligations (which result in a just order) on the other? Two factors need to be considered in answering this question. The first is the weight, or seriousness, to be attached to the freedoms and obligations at stake. Freedoms and obligations are not all equal: they can be ranked according to the degree to which they increase or diminish one's freedom and opportunities. Clearly, the right to life ranks much higher than the right or opportunity to establish and run a manufacturing plant in the way that one thinks is most effective and efficient. Thus if my manufacturing process results in toxic, carcinogenic chemicals contaminating others' water supply, it would clearly be just to enact a law that protects the public's health—even their lives—by requiring me to carefully dispose of the toxic waste. The relative importance of the competing freedoms and obligations is one crucial factor to be weighed in determining what is just.

A second factor that can sometimes help, particularly in cases in which the first factor gives no clear direction, is comparing the number of people who will win certain freedoms with the number who will be assigned corresponding obligations. If the freedoms and obligations being apportioned are roughly equal in importance, but many more people will find their freedoms restricted by additional obligations than will find their freedoms increased by additional opportunities, justice would say that the apportionment is not equitable.

In the early 1980s Michigan's Department of Social Services began to develop a new system in Detroit, designed in part to assure that people in the Medicaid program receive medical care. care. A crisis had been brewing because of the very large number of poor people receiving medical care under the Medicaid program and the increasing number of doctors who, for a variety of reasons, were refusing to see Medicaid recipients. As a result, a growing number of poor were finding it increasingly difficult to obtain care from their own personal physicians and had to seek treatment at central city hospitals and clinics. Some unscrupulous doctors were making enormous profits from the program by taking on huge caseloads of patients and giving them only minimal care. So a plan was developed that required every Medicaid patient to sign up with a specific physician selected from a group of physicians who had agreed to participate in this new program. The patient was guaranteed access to this physician but could go to this physician only (unless referred by him or her to another physician).

The new opportunities for most of the Medicaid patients were clear: they were guaranteed access to their own physician, whereas before they had often ended up at a low-quality "Medicaid mill" clinic. Yet this plan also meant that some Medicaid patients who previously had been able to move freely from one physician to another could no longer do so. Especially those relatively few Medicaid patients who lived in more affluent areas with a large number of physicians suffered some loss of free choice. But most Medicaid patients gained new opportunities through the guaranteed-access system—opportunities that many, especially those living in the inner city, did not have before. Because many people gained new freedoms or opportunities and a relatively small number of people had their freedom of choice restricted, I would argue that the plan was just.

As the next section makes abundantly clear, it is often very difficult to determine in specific, concrete situations exactly what is just. It is a process of balancing and weighing, a process that requires personal judgment and discretion. This difficult task can be made more manageable, however, by considering both the importance of the freedoms and obligations at stake and the number of people who will be affected by the balance being shifted in one direction or another.

One final point. Achieving the balance between opportunities and obligations that results in a just order would be a natural, lighthearted, joyous task if men and women were the perfect beings originally created by God. But something has gone tragically wrong in human affairs. Humankind is marked by sin and its bitter fruit, listed in Galatians: "sexual immorality, impurity and debauchery; idolatry and witchcraft; hatred, discord, jealousy, fits of rage, selfish ambition, dissensions, factions and envy; drunkenness, orgies, and the like" (5:19–21). The natural result of sin is that men and women demand more and more for themselves and recognize fewer and fewer obligations they owe others. The consequences are societies that constantly veer off the proper track and support unjust orders marked by exploitation of the poor, oppression of minority races, and destruction of the natural environment. More powerful societies take advantage of weaker societies. Disorder and injustices that would prevent people from living the joyful, loving, creative lives God intends for all his children constantly threaten to become the prevailing condition of humankind.

It is because of this constant tendency of societies to succumb to unjust orders that God has established governments to oppose evil and to promote justice. In light of the nature of a just order, this means that government has the God-given task of balancing freedoms and obligations in such a way that it increases people's opportunities to live lives of praise to God and service to others. The sinfulness of the human heart makes this task both tremendously important and tremendously difficult. Let no one underestimate either aspect of it.

JUSTICE IN THE POLITICAL WORLD

We have completed a long but necessary detour and now are ready to tackle the question of whether or not to require motorcyclists to wear helmets—as well as the millions of other specific, concrete questions of zoning, taxation, racial and sexual discrimination, environmental regulation, welfare, and other public policies that the various levels of government struggle with daily. Our detour led us to the basic conclusion that Christians should work for a more just order in society by supporting those policy alternatives that strike a proper balance between freedoms and obligations. Now the problem is how to take this vision down into the swirling world of political issues and events and apply it thoughtfully and consistently.

Justice: no magic formula. One thing must be made clear from the start: two people who agree on using this standard to determine their positions on political issues and questions will often still arrive at opposite conclusions. It is not a magic formula leading irresistibly to preordained answers. It is a standard, a yardstick, but applying it to current, concrete issues is a creative process rather than a mechanical one.

Two specific factors often lead people equally committed to following the standard of justice to arrive at different conclusions. The first is incomplete information. In the real world one never operates on the basis of knowing all the facts. Usually, big chunks of information crucial to making a thoughtful, conscientious decision are missing completely or, at best, are fuzzy and in dispute.

An ongoing controversy in Michigan concerns whether or not the state should grant the United States Navy an easement on state forestland so that it can build a radio-antenna grid with which to communicate with submarines equipped with nuclear missiles. Part of the controversy involves the question of whether or not the radio waves to be sent out by the antenna would pose a health threat to people living nearby. Some studies indicate that there may be some health risks, especially increased chances of developing leukemia. But these studies are far from conclusive, and their methodologies are badly flawed, not coming close to replicating the situation that would be created by the Navy's proposed radio grid. The preponderance of evidence seems to indicate that the radio grid is not a health hazard, or at least is no greater a health hazard than that created by many electrical transmission lines or found in many workplaces. Yet some doubt remains. Facts are in dispute.

Clearly, if the antenna would pose a real and present danger to nearby residents, justice would oppose the project and tell the Navy to find some safer way to communicate with its submarines. But that is not the case. The danger is small and uncertain—but how small and how uncertain is not known. In such situations it becomes understandable why two equally sincere, equally dedicated individuals, both of whom are equally committed to using biblical justice as their standard, may reach opposite conclusions.

Yet almost every political issue in the real world of people and events must be decided in the face of missing information. Only rarely does the decision-maker enjoy the luxury of basing a conclusion on complete information.

Also helping to explain why our standard of biblical justice is not a mechanical standard leading to fixed, predetermined results is the fact that one relevant value often clashes with another. Applying the standard involves a weighing or balancing process. Freedoms and obligations are being apportioned. What values are at stake and what weight they should be given are often at the heart of political issues.

Let's say that one had perfect knowledge of the radio-grid issue—knew that the radio antenna would cause, say, one person a year to die of leukemia but also would create a thousand new jobs in a high-poverty area with twenty-two percent unemployment, and, by improving our control over submarines equipped with nuclear missiles, would reduce the chances of an accidental nuclear war starting by one one-hundredth of a percent. Still, the position that best promotes justice would not be totally clear or obvious. How does one weigh the liberating change that would brighten the lives of the thousand families whose wage earners would now find meaningful employment— perhaps for the first time in years—against the tragedy of a few families who would face the death of one of their members, and then weigh both against even the slightest reduction in the chances of the ultimate tragedy of nuclear war? Given this situation, reasonable, equally committed people could reach different conclusions—this time because of different assessments of the importance of the competing values.

In summary, political issues are not resolved in a quiet, pristine, laboratory-like world where complete information is available and people have the time to carefully sort out and weigh the relevant values. Typically, information is incomplete, values clash, and time is short. Given these circumstances, it is hardly surprising that even people who start out with the same biblical standard sometimes end up disagreeing.

But even when they do disagree, their disagreement is on a much higher level—and therefore much has been gained—than those disagreements that occur because of false standards or selfish ambitions. Two politically involved people with the same biblical standard who are struggling over an issue are not like a couple of alley cats fighting and snarling over a scrap of food; they are more like two neighbors who disagree and have sat down to try to work out a mutually satisfactory solution. The debate is on a much higher plane, and the chances of a reasonable solution that will lead to creating a more just order are much greater than if the debate were based on fundamental disagreements about goals and purposes.

Moral politics versus the politics of justice.　Sometimes a distinction is made between moral issues, on which Christians are presumed to have something distinctive to offer, and morally neutral issues, on which Christians are presumed to have ideas neither more nor less noteworthy than anyone else's. In this view, public-policy issues such as abortion, pornography, prayer in the schools, and gay rights are usually seen as moral issues, and presumably other issues are seen as morally neutral. Some would add such issues as poverty, nuclear disarmament, unemployment, and environmental pollution to the list of moral issues about which Christians should be deeply concerned.

In both cases, however, people seem to start out with the assumption that if something is morally right and good, it is the proper role of government to impose it on all of society. The first group tends to latch onto personal ethics and the second group onto social ethics; the first group thereby runs into greater dangers, but both groups would be on firmer ground if they began by asking what is just instead of what is moral. The two are related, but they are distinct, and the distinction can make a huge difference. Christianity teaches us that government is to pursue justice, and thus Christians have a moral duty to pursue justice in the political world. Being a morally ethical Christian entails seeking public or political justice. But this does not mean that all morality is justice. Christians must remember that they are called to hold certain private, personal standards of morality that have little to do with political justice.

Government is to pursue justice, not morality apart from justice. To the extent that justice and morality overlap, one can say that the justice-promoting activities of government are also promoting morality, but it is the pursuit of justice that is the controlling factor, not the pursuit of morality apart from justice.

The difficulty of government pursuing morality apart from justice is made apparent by the basic fact that no one can be forced to be good, to be moral, since morality is a matter of the inner self, the heart, and governments can deal only with outward actions. Government can, for example, deter a man from killing his neighbor by threatening him with imprisonment or even death. But our Lord has told us that anyone who hates his neighbor has already committed murder in his heart. Thus government can stop an individual from acting out the dark hatred within his or her heart, but this involves no moral improvement in God's sight if the feeling that would motivate the deed is still there.

Similarly, when in the past Christians have possessed a majority of political power, they have often passed Sunday-observance laws that have closed stores, outlawed sporting events, and sometimes even required church attendance. Whatever one may think of such laws, let us be clear on one thing: they have little to do with morality. If "keeping the Sabbath day holy" means worshiping God in church, abstaining from commercial activities and sports, and devoting the day to spiritual growth and study, Sunday "blue laws" have little to do with true Sunday observance. The person who would have gone shopping or to a ball game on Sunday if such activities were not legally banned is likely to spend Sunday paying bills or playing pool in the basement—activities fully as commercial or recreational as the more public but outlawed ones. The government can even force a person to attend church, but it can force no one to worship God. People forced to sit in a church service, who then spend the time scheming or nursing hateful grudges, are hardly worshiping God!

Morality is a matter of the heart. And no law, no government can control that. Justice is a matter of overt acts, and that is what government can and should control.

Justice and morality ask two quite different questions.

Justice asks, "Does this issue involve questions of freedom and opportunity?" and "What position, on balance, would give more people greater freedom and opportunity to live fuller, more joyful, more creative lives?" Morality asks, "Does this issue involve questions of morally good behavior?"

Moral politics is, in essence, totalitarian. It seeks to control people, to force them to be good—or at least to force them to maintain the outward appearances of good behavior, since this is all moral politics can in actuality accomplish.

The politics of justice, on the other hand, is liberating and pluralistic. It is liberating in the sense that it seeks greater freedom and opportunity, not stifling conformity to someone's concept of moral behavior. The result of this freedom is pluralism. Different individuals and groups will respond to their own faith commitments—whether those of Christianity, Judaism, humanism, or hedonism. God wills that all women and men love him and obey his commandments, but he wills that this love and obedience be freely given to him—not exacted from people through the power of law.

Some, given the freedom to choose whether or not to obey, will not. This means a pluralistic society in which some will pursue activities, form organizations, and express opinions contrary to those that Christians would pursue, form, and express. There will be mosques as well as churches, nudist camps as well as Bible camps, hateful, racist literature as well as the writings of a C. S. Lewis and a Martin Luther King, Jr.

Yet justice with the resulting pluralism is not anarchistic. It does not say that we all can do what we like irrespective of the impact on others. Justice recognizes that we live in society and that one person's actions can have a profound effect on others' freedoms—thus the importance of assuring rights and opportunities through the process of balancing freedom and obligations.

Take, for example, religion in the public schools. The politics of justice opposes with equal fervor actions that would either mandate or outlaw prayers or other religious exercises in the public schools. It therefore would oppose public prayers or other religious exercises as part of classroom activities, even though such activities are highly moral and even required by God. Christmas—or, for that matter, holidays of other religions—should not be observed. The differing religious backgrounds of the students' families and justice's concern for the freedom of these students and their families demand this much.

But the politics of justice also opposes some recent court decisions that have outlawed the use of school facilities for voluntary religious activities outside normal school hours. Such politics would also allow the teaching of Christian and other religious views on such topics as the origins of the earth and humankind, obedience to government, and social problems. If such rights are not asserted, public schools can become the enemy of religion, stifling the freedom to act on one's religious beliefs that justice demands. There is in fact a danger that the public schools in the United States today, instead of being genuinely pluralistic, will teach a faith commitment—some would say religion—that is outside of any recognized formal religion but is based on a perceived consensual, materialistic, nontheistic "Americanism." But the public schools should be pluralistic institutions, not melting pots. They should allow for a colorful diversity of religious commitments, not promote a homogenized, secular faith.

In contrast, moral politics sees prayer as good and therefore something to be promoted or even required in the public schools. It seeks—in its Christian manifestations—to make the public schools into Christian schools. After all, we are a Christian nation, are we not? In some ways we are indeed a Christian nation. And I would to God we were much more deeply a Christian nation—that more of our people were committed, obedient Christians, that our great universities such as Yale, Harvard, and Princeton reflected a Christian understanding of learning as they once did, and that our political leaders openly acknowledged Jesus Christ as Savior and Lord. But this is quite different from saying that our nation should be "Christian" by using political power to force nonChristians—including children in the public schools who come from nonChristian families—to exhibit the outward signs of Christian belief. That is neither justice nor Christianity; it is totalitarianism. And that is precisely where moral politics leads us.

But after having taken all this time to distinguish moral politics and the politics of justice, I would like to make some final comments which in some important ways bring the two concepts close together. If by "moral politics" we mean politics based on Christian morality, that morality is summed up in the commands to love God above all and our neighbors as ourselves. The Bible testifies that this is indeed what lies at the heart of true Christian morality. The Christian political activist should in fact be guided and motivated by this vision of morality. My only point is that in the political world that love of God and neighbor must show itself in a passion for a more just order. One loves God and one's fellows, and therefore he or she seeks justice for them.

How does one show love, for example, to prostitutes, many of whom have been led into this degrading means of making a living by an unjust, male-dominated society? The contention that most prostitutes freely chose this occupation is a thinly disguised fiction. Does one then show love to the prostitute by legalizing prostitution on the grounds that justice does not seek to impose a single moral standard of behavior on everyone, but instead allows for a variety of life-styles and moral choices? I think not. In a world of sexism, racism, exploitive pimps, and macho-influenced males, prostitution is usually nothing more than the ultimate in sexual exploitation and has nothing to do with the joyful, loving, creative life of which the Bible's vision of justice speaks.

The politics of justice—if it is motivated by a true love for all God's children and rests on a sophisticated vision of justice—will work, insistently and constantly, for a world of justice in which moral lives exhibiting love for God and humankind are made possible and encouraged. It creates the room an individual needs to live a moral life of love. Paradoxically, the politics of justice thereby attains, in a deeper and more profound sense, a higher level of morality than moral politics, with its direct pursuit of morality through the use of political power.

Justice: part of every issue. There are implications for justice in every issue that government deals with. One of the problems with confusing morality with justice as the guiding principle of political action arises from the fact that "morality"—in the sense that clear Christian ethical issues are directly involved—is often not present in political issues. Thus if morality as such were the standard, Christianity would not speak to many political issues.

But justice is present in all political issues. It is a more inclusive standard than morality. Political decisions by their very nature assign freedoms and obligations, benefits and costs in society. Political decisions do not have neutral effects: each decision has its winners and its losers. This is often true in a monetary sense, as it is when certain taxes are raised and others lowered, certain contracts are awarded, or more money is appropriated for one purpose and less for another. But there can also be winners and losers in terms of values or beliefs, as when schools are allowed or forbidden to offer classes in sex education, abortions are restricted or made more freely available, or reciting the pledge of allegiance is made mandatory at the start of each school day. In these examples—taken from actual political controversies—some financial advantages or disadvantages are part of the issue, but they are far outweighed (for most people involved) by the values or beliefs that are being affirmed or denied.

As we saw earlier, justice means striking a balance between freedoms and obligations, and doing so in a way that increases the opportunities available to all to live loving, joyful, creative lives. Since political decisions consistently involve assigning freedoms and obligations, benefits and costs—thus creating a social order that is more just or less just—they consistently involve justice.

Justice will often be involved only indirectly, and, as stressed earlier in this chapter, specific decisions will often affect the level of justice present in society to a very small degree. Yet justice is there. The Christian political activist who is justice-oriented will constantly be alert for the implications for justice in the issues that he or she is dealing with. For it is these small, incremental, often seemingly inconsequential steps toward or away from justice that determine the level of justice present in a society.

The politics of justice versus individualistic politics.   One of the tendencies of many politically aware people that can lead to difficulties is that of seeing social and political issues almost totally in individualistic terms. An entirely appropriate emphasis on the importance of the individual can—and in the American experience frequently does—blind one to recognizing that individuals do not live, work, and play as separate beings. Instead, society is a whole made up of individuals who are grouped into innumerable organic associations. Individuals can fulfill their God-given purpose as thinking, willing, joyful, creative beings only as parts of families, circles of friends, churches or synagogues, neighborhoods, work groups, clubs, unions, and countless other groupings. Very few human activities are done alone. Normally we eat, learn, work, play, and worship together. And usually we do so with people with whom we share not a fleeting acquaintance but a continuing relationship.

Therefore, in determining what is just in specific, concrete situations, one must be sensitive to how the options one faces will affect these groups or associations. Justice is not merely an individualistic concept. It recognizes the group dimension that is vital both to human well-being and to a just order.

The mainstream of American liberal thought often emphasizes individual rights, which are seen in isolation from the rights or benefits the individual possesses as part of a group. As a result, justice is sometimes not promoted. For justice to be truly just, the freedoms and opportunities a person enjoys as part of a group or association must be recognized.

Let me illustrate what I mean. I once introduced a bill in the Michigan Senate that would permit cities with a municipal income-tax to adopt ordinances allowing taxpayers living in a section of the city with a formally organized neighborhood association to designate one dollar of their income taxes to go to that association. I had expected opposition from the municipal bureaucracies, which often had been the object of unwanted pressures from neighborhood associations. I had also expected opposition from some conservatives who might see neighborhood associations as radical, pro-change forces. But most of my opposition came from two of the most liberal members of the Senate. They argued that we ought not to subsidize neighborhood associations because they sometimes violated the rights of others, as when they tried to keep low-income housing out of their neighborhoods or tried to maintain the ethnic character of their neighborhoods. I readily agreed that neighborhood associations had sometimes taken stances that could be disapproved of on those grounds and that were in fact simply selfish and wrong. But I felt that this was no reason to deny cities the option of allowing neighborhood associations an additional means to raise funds.

Neighborhoods are extremely important groupings in which people can find identity, meaning, and self-fulfillment in the values, friendships, and identifications fostered in an organic, closely knit atmosphere. If a just order is defined as one that allows people the freedoms and opportunities to find fulfillment and meaning, then the protection, encouragement, and strengthening of strong neighborhoods constitute one important way to achieve a more just order in our large, necessarily impersonal cities. Anti-discrimination laws already provided legal sanctions against overt acts of discrimination based on race, religion, ethnicity, income, or occupation. With these safeguards in place, I felt that the fears of the two liberal senators were largely based on an overly individualistic view of society. They did not see neighborhoods as being important to achieving the freedoms and opportunities that define justice.

In this view, all ethnic, religious, and other such distinctions are blurred or reduced to insignificance. It sees all people living together in a single huge society without finding meaning and identity in smaller, more personal associations or groups. This vision of society is not pluralistic but individualistic. By refusing to recognize the natural, organic groupings in society, it refuses to recognize the social nature of humankind and our need to find our purpose in company with small groups of like-minded people. A just social order recognizes the importance of such associations and groups, and therefore promotes them or at the very least does not work against them.

Should we then require motorcyclists to wear safety helmets? By now it is clear that neither the Bible nor even the biblically based vision of justice I have developed offers a clear-cut, obvious answer to that question. Yet what I have presented in this chapter speaks directly to the question. The "bikers" were right: whether or not they should be required to wear helmets is a question of justice. The standard ought not to be what I personally believe would be the morally responsible thing for me to do if I were to ride a motorcycle. The question should be resolved by reference to freedoms and obligations that lead to opportunities for all God's children to lead joyful, loving, creative lives of praise and service. And justice must weigh the impact the decision will have on families and other social groupings, not only consider how it will affect the individual.

But after all is said and done—whether it is the question of motorcyclists wearing helmets or weightier questions of racial discrimination, food for the hungry, or war and peace—Christians must make individual decisions on the issues. It is only through personal struggles with their own consciences—which have been informed by the teachings of the Bible, by their own understanding of the world, by the help of the broader church, and by the guidance of the Holy Spirit—that they can answer on what side of the constant stream of decisions flowing by them justice demands they should stand.

4

REDEEMING
THE POLITICAL PROCESS

"Dirty politics" is a phrase that is almost as common as "Merry Christmas." In fact, we have a whole stable full of terms with negative connotations that we often use instead of neutral terms to describe political phenomena: "smoke-filled rooms" instead of "conference rooms," "political hacks" instead of "political workers," and "political machines" instead of "political organizations."

From my own experience I can testify that, in fact, the political process is often seamy and even sordid. On certain days when I was in the middle of a political campaign or struggling to win or stop passage of a particular bill, I was reminded of Paul's words in Ephesians: "Our struggle is not against flesh and blood, but against the rulers, against the authorities, against the powers of this dark world and against the spiritual forces of evil in the heavenly realms" (6:12). Not that the individuals whom I worked with and whom I was sometimes pitted against were especially evil people or schemers with unusually corrupt motives. Most of them were ordinary, seemingly decent people.

The problem is that the system taken as a whole—the entire interlocking network of attitudes and expectations that permeate our political institutions and practices—creates an atmosphere where such ideals as justice, righteousness, order, and servant-hood are absent. Thus those who struggle for these ideals do not face their biggest challenge from some particularly dramatic, clearly labeled evil but from nebulous, all-pervasive attitudes and expectations. Evil is everywhere and nowhere. It is everywhere in that it is pervasive and ever-present; it is nowhere in that it can come to appear so natural and so much a part of the political atmosphere that is goes unnoticed, like the air we breathe. The God-inspired political struggle for greater justice thereby becomes a spiritual struggle against "the powers of this dark world."

This means that the person committed to working politically for a more just order will often be struggling against seemingly all-powerful, intractable forces, forces of parochial self-interest, ponderous inertia, and organized special interests. But at other times the bigger struggle will be the personal inward one. Then the temptation will be to move away from one's own ideals and standards of behavior one small step at a time.

Later in this chapter I describe some of the specific forms that political temptations and wrongdoing can take, but there is one common thread that runs through them all: using one's own selfish ambitions as one's chief guiding standard. The kind of political system that we have structured in our nation is most likely to reward those who have put their own selfish ambitions at the center of their lives. In fact, almost everyone in the system—other legislators, lobbyists, political aides, reporters, and campaign consultants—expects politicians to be concerned about their own reelection, to seek publicity for themselves, and to avoid taking stances that will hurt their standing with the public. This is the way things are done—this is politics! No one expects them to act differently.

But the Apostle James has written about selfish ambition and its bitter fruit in his description of the two different kinds of wisdom (3:13–18). One kind of "wisdom," based on "bitter envy and selfish ambition," is earthly and demonic. The actions that spring from it will result in "disorder and every evil practice." I have often turned to this passage when I have been in the middle of an especially difficult political struggle and have wryly thought that James must have had congressional campaigns or Michigan politics in mind when he wrote these words! Selfish ambition is all too often the norm: legislators frequently try to increase their own political power by stretching the truth past the point of deception, by taking credit for a bill they had very little to do with passing, by advocating popular positions that are silly at best and harmful to many at worst, or by fighting to get a key position of legislative leadership and then not doing the work necessary to use it to accomplish needed reforms. It is out of such quests for power that, according to James, "disorder and every evil practice" result.

But the second kind of wisdom that James writes about comes from God and is "first of all pure; then peace loving, considerate, submissive, full of mercy and good fruit, impartial and sincere." The result of such wisdom is righteousness, or, as the New English Bible translates it, justice. And that is the wisdom of the Christian political activist: to be pure in motive; to seek peace with all people; to be considerate of others, willing to be submissive instead of constantly seeking the spotlight; to be merciful and impartial and fair; and to be sincere in all words and actions.

Each of these characteristics seems to be the exact opposite of that of the stereotypical politician. We expect politicians to replace purity with compromise; to win by being confrontational and intimidating rather than peaceful, considerate, and submissive; to seek publicity instead of avoiding the spotlight; to drive ruthlessly for their personal goals instead of demonstrating mercy and impartiality; and to stretch the truth and to hide their true motives instead of being honest in what they say and do.

In the previous chapters I have spoken of justice and order as the basic, God-given purpose of government. I spent much time explaining how and why I am convinced that this is the basic purpose of government and why this is the basic reason for Christian political involvement. In addition, I discussed at length the nature of justice and the questions one must ask when applying justice in concrete, specific situations. But having been active in politics for ten years, I can testify that such considerations are far removed from the everyday workings of legislative bodies and election campaigns.

Two totally separate worlds seem to appear: the world of self-giving biblical wisdom and ideals, where justice, order, freedom, and righteousness hold sway; and the "real world," where compromise, pressure, ruthlessness, threats, and selfish ambitions prevail. Each world appears irrelevant to the other—

and in fact they often are. But this is a description of a disease, not of the world as it should be or must be.

My point is that powerful forces are present in our political system that, if left to themselves without the redeeming grace of God, naturally result in seamy, sordid politics. I use the word "naturally," but they are a natural result only in the sense that a cancer growing in a human body will, if untreated, naturally lead to total corruption and eventual death. That cancer is anything but natural in the sense of being right and proper and necessarily present. Similarly, a politics that is divorced from considerations of justice, purpose, and meaning is anything but natural. It may be the form that politics usually takes in our world, but that does not change the fact that it is an aberration. In the cancer ward of a large hospital it may seem natural to have cancer, and someone mistakenly placed in the ward might even appear to be some strange aberration. But we who know what a healthy, cancer-free body is like know that such a person should be the norm, the standard that others in the ward, through proper treatment, might someday reach.

Similarly, Christians know what politics should be. We are called to redeem politics in the name of Jesus Christ, empowered to transform, not to be conformed to the world of politics as it is.

In this chapter I first consider three false ways that Christians sometimes use to try to close the gap between the world of politics as it is and as it should be. Then I consider five basic characteristics of the political process, examining the form these characteristics "naturally" take in their fallen state, and exploring how Christians are called to redeem them for our Lord.

POLITICS AS IT IS AND AS IT SHOULD BE: FALSE PATHS TO CLOSING THE GAP

Testify but avoid direct involvement. In light of the gap between politics as it is and politics as it should be, some Christians have chosen to testify against the evils in the political system but to avoid actually participating directly in the political process, since they believe it is wrong to engage in the compromises and moral corruptions they see as inherent in the process. Those who take this approach recognize correctly that the church of

Jesus Christ must be concerned about and involved in politics. Christians indeed have much to say to the political world about righteousness and justice. But those with this approach also see the political world as being so corrupt and so corrupting—they especially see the pursuit of power itself as corrupting—that they believe Christians should testify to the political world from outside it. Christians are to speak to the government—sometimes speaking through the direct challenges of demonstrations and even civil disobedience—but they are to avoid the moral compromises seen as intrinsic to direct participation in politics. The church is called to testify and to prophesy—through words, demonstrations, and the creation of alternative communities that show what it means to be in Christ fully and unconditionally. Thus one can in fact be an agent for change in the political world and still be true to God.

Certainly God can use Christians to testify to the political world from outside it, and has called some to do so. Nothing is wrong in that. In fact, there is much good in it. The church needs to confront the political world with its evil practices, selfish pursuits, and unjust public policies.

But the church must not stop there. God calls some Christians—some of his church—to work directly in politics. Seeking to redeem a political world without Christians participating in it is neither necessary nor effective. It is not necessary because one can be in the world but not of the world—and that holds for the political world, too. As I explained in Chapter Two, government and politics are by nature good. They are ordained and established by God as his agents of justice and order on earth. Government and politics are good institutions that have fallen—as have the family, the church, and other such human institutions. There is nothing *inherently* evil about government and politics. Thus there is no necessary, inherent reason to avoid direct, personal political involvement.

If the political world were inherently evil, that would change the situation. A young Christian woman who feels called by God to minister to the prostitutes of a large city ought not to become a prostitute herself in order to improve the effectiveness of her witness, because prostitution is inherently and necessarily contrary to God's will. But politics does not fit into such a category. It is good, righteous, and noble, although admittedly fallen and therefore corrupted.

Moreover, trying to redeem the political world from the outside is not effective—or at least not as effective as working to change politics from within. Some things can be done only from the inside. One can fully understand the political world only by directly participating in it. In addition, it is crucial to have at least some people within government leading the way and demonstrating by their very lives the new way that Christians are proclaiming. Remember, even Jesus Christ was a direct participant: he saved our world not by testifying to us from outside it but by becoming one of us. The church must identify with the worlds it seeks to redeem as fully as Jesus Christ identified with us and our needy, suffering world. That means a part of the church—some Christians—must participate directly in politics, identifying with those making up the political world and showing the meaning of Christian political service in the way they live and work.

In fact, it is contradictory to testify to those in government, urging them to follow paths of greater justice, and at the same time to believe that Christians themselves ought not to participate in government. Remember that government consists of fellow human beings holding a host of political offices, and that when one testifies to the government one testifies to these people. If a person truly believes that men and women ought not to be directly engaged in political activity—pursuing and holding political power over others—his or her only consistent witness to those in political office can be to call them to abandon this work and take up other pursuits. To do otherwise would be the same as calling a prostitute not to abandon her profession but to serve God as a prostitute. Either one must recognize the possibility and appropriateness of people serving God in politics, or one must urge everyone to leave political office. There is no other choice.

Be a suffering failure. A second approach sometimes taken by Christians concerned about the disparity between politics as it is and as it should be is to decide to enter the political arena directly, but to do so resigned to being unable to build any significant political influence. Those who take this approach assume that the evil of the political world is so great that the only way one can build influence within it is to compromise in such a way as to be unfaithful to one's commitment to Jesus Christ. Thus one enters politics but sees his or her lack of success almost as proof that one is being faithful to Christ. Failure can become a source of pride. The situation is much like that of a missionary to the Muslims of the Middle East or North Africa who goes because he or she feels called, but who learns not to expect success and soon gives up on even trying to devise methods that will increase success. Eventually one may become proud of this failure, taking it as a proof that one is being faithful to the gospel, that one is not watering it down.

There is a grain of truth and a mountain of error in such an approach. The grain of truth is that God does indeed call Christians first of all to be faithful, not to be successful. Christians are to offer God faithful service, and it is up to him to decide how to use it. It may please him to take a certain individual in a particular time and use his or her political service to accomplish what most of us would call success: mountains of injustice, oppression, and war will give way to justice, freedom, and peace. Others equally faithful and equally dedicated may find God using their offered political service to accomplish very few concrete, visible results.

Hebrews 11 speaks first of all of the heroes of faith who conquered kingdoms, established justice, and escaped dangers (32–38). But then without a pause it goes on to describe equally faithful people who were put to death or ignored. Both groups were heroes of faith; both offered equally acceptable service to God. But it was God who decided what use to make of the service they offered him.

So it is for those who enter the political arena—or any other arena, for that matter—to serve God. They should not expect failure; they should work persistently and doggedly for success. But ultimately it is up to God to decide, in his sovereignty and grace, how best to employ his servants' efforts. Christians are called to be faithful—not to be either successes or failures.

The mountain of error that looms in the belief that the faithful Christian public servant is doomed to be a minor political influence can be seen in the testimony of events and history. Time and again events have shown that there is no reason to expect that God will never—or only rarely—use the service of politically involved Christians to achieve greater justice. Think of William Wilberforce in early nineteenth-century England and his fellow evangelical members of Parliament, who played a key role in abolishing the English slave trade and in achieving other social reforms. In our own day one might think of Senator Mark Hatfield and Congressman Don Bonker, whose Christian testimonies are clear and whose struggles to enact more just policies are often successful. Countless other sincere, dedicated evangelical Christians work daily in Congress, in state legislatures and local councils, and on judicial benches throughout the country. Certainly God is blessing their efforts and using them to achieve greater justice.

The point in all this is that under current political conditions in America, Christians can be fully true to their Savior and yet succeed politically by winning positions of influence and then using these positions to achieve more just public policies. It can be done. I claim no more—and no less.

Do evil to accomplish a greater good.   A third approach to the gap between politics as it is and as it should be is to acknowledge that to be actively involved in politics one will have to compromise his or her moral standards, but that this is a necessary sacrifice made in order that greater good may result. Those who argue this position usually begin by giving an extreme example, such as whether or not it would be defensible for a father to lie to a rapist who has broken into his house and is looking for his daughter. His daughter is hiding in a concealed closet upstairs, yet he tells the would-be rapist that he is home alone.

Most of us would acknowledge that the father's action was morally proper. True, the father purposely misled the rapist and the Bible clearly says, "Do not bear false witness against your neighbor." But it is equally true that the Bible's commands, although absolute and true, are not to be followed in a wooden, mindless fashion. The Bible and our Lord time and again teach us that the basic principle underlying all of the more specific commands of the Bible is love (see Matt. 22:37–40 and Rom. 13:8–10).

Thus the father trapped in the circumstances of the example would be fully justified in telling the rapist his daughter was not at home. In fact, to do otherwise would be wrong. To help the rapist in his sinful sexual violence by revealing the hiding-place of his intended victim is not showing love to him, and it surely is not showing love to her.

But this kind of reasoning would lead some to conclude that in politics, too, people must be allowed to make their accommodations to evil so that they can continue to serve in political office and accomplish the good that their positions enable them to. But this is wrong. There is no room in Christian ethics for an "ends justifies the means" approach apart from the law of love, and that is what this approach really is. It says, "Do evil— act unlovingly toward others as you strike your compromises with evil—so that good ends can be achieved. After all, isn't a little deception or chicanery all right if it means the poor will have greater opportunities to live lives of creative joy and peace?"

But this reasoning is entirely different from the reasoning in the example of the father who misleads the rapist. For in that case the "lie" was in itself the loving act, and therefore the morally appropriate thing to do. It was not a matter of doing an unloving thing so that some other good would result.

My point can be illustrated by another example. In this case there is a father whose daughter has not been taking reasonable precautions against sexual assault—perhaps she has been walking alone at night in a neighborhood with a history of sexual assaults. So the father tries to frighten her into behaving more responsibly by purposely exaggerating the danger and the lawlessness of the people living in that particular neighborhood. When confronted with his exaggerations, the father readily admits that he has been trying to instill some fear in his daughter with his less-than-truthful accounts, but he justifies them on the basis of the desired end: to spare his daughter from sexual assault by changing her behavior. "Anything less wouldn't have affected her. I had to do it for her own good," he explains.

The two examples I have used share some similarities. In both cases the father used deception in an attempt to spare his daughter the horror of a sexual assault. In both cases the deception may have had the positive result desired. But the kinds of deception involved were crucially different. In the first case the deception itself was an act of love done for all concerned. In the second case the end was good but the means were evil. An entire neighborhood and its residents were slandered—no love at all was shown to them—and the daughter was tricked into changing her behavior. In the end, then, the father did not show love or respect to his daughter, either.

The evil some would argue one can do in the political world in order to achieve a greater good is much closer to that of the second example than the first. In fact, I cannot think of a single example, either from my personal experience or from my wide reading about political life, in which a case of the first nature arose. The instances are always of the second type, as when one is tempted to vote against an unpopular bill, even though it is badly needed, in order to avoid being vulnerable to attack during the next election. "Why not do evil—vote against a bill that I know is needed—to accomplish a greater good? I'll be reelected and then I can continue to do good on even more important matters." This kind of thinking is wrong. If God wants you back in office, you will be reelected even if you vote for the bill.

The slope of doing "small evils" that much greater good can be achieved is a slippery one. Small step by small step, one can soon find oneself wallowing in the mire of selfish ambition. We are called to redeem politics, not to make accommodations to politics as usual.

After reviewing these three paths to resolving the gap between politics as it should be and as it is, the politically concerned Christian is no further along. The gap is still unbridged.

Yet I am convinced of two things: (1) God calls Christians to be deeply and actively involved in the political process, and (2) God does not will anyone to be involved in immoral practices or to be guided by selfish ambitions. There must be another way, a way to be actively involved in politics so that the very process of politics itself—the way the Christian pursues political power and political justice—is redeemed. The Christian is called to redeem politics by living a life of Christian obedience in the midst of a system that has quite different expectations, quite different standards of behavior. In the process one closes the gap between politics as it is and as it should be—not by avoiding direct political involvements, not by resigning oneself to an inability to achieve political influence, and not by making accommodations to the evil aspects of politics—but by living a life of faithful service in the midst of what often is a wasteland of selfish ambition. One can hope that others will follow one's example and testimony, but whether or not they do, he or she is faithful.

In the remaining portion of this chapter I consider five basic characteristics of the political process in the United States. For each I consider the form it "naturally" takes in its unredeemed state, controlled by selfish ambitions, and the form it takes in its redeemed state, controlled by a commitment to serving God by pursuing justice. In the process I hope to shed more light on the nature of the political world and what it means for Christians to be active in it.

POLITICS AS COMBAT

Political decisions are decisions that deeply affect the lives and values of people and groups in society. How justice is defined in a given situation—what freedoms are or are not protected and what opportunities are or are not assured—can profoundly affect people in direct, personal ways—as when a government contract is gained or lost and employment or unemployment results, or a toxic-waste dump is or is not built in one's neighborhood. How justice is defined can also have a profound effect in terms of values—as when abortions are allowed in the face of strong feelings that abortion is murder.

Because vitally important decisions are made in the face of sharply divergent views, struggle or combat results. The nineteenth-century Prussian general Clausewitz once defined war as politics by other means. One can just as well define politics as war by other means. Politics is a peaceful means to resolve conflicts—but that does not remove any of the struggle associated with warfare.

Because the stakes are often very high in politics, people's willingness to expend prodigious amounts of time, money, and energy is equally high. An unsuccessful state Senate candidate in my hometown recently had to sell his house to pay off campaign debts. The Watergate scandal demonstrated vividly the lengths to which people will go to fight for persons and causes they believe in. There are numerous instances of legislators leaving sickbeds against their doctors' orders to make crucial roll-call votes. People regularly risk health, financial security, and family in order to pursue political goals.

In its unredeemed state the combativeness of politics can easily degenerate into a struggle dominated by people's selfish ambitions marked by nothing more substantive than macho swagger. The political world is largely a male world dominated by people whose primary goals are all too often getting reelected (or elected), amassing greater personal power and commanding the ego-satisfying deference and perks that come with political power, and even enjoying the sublimated violence of political combat. I have often been struck by the frequent use of violent— often sexually violent—metaphors in legislative cloakrooms and campaign-strategy meetings.

If a person is not clearly and self-consciously committed to pursuing his or her vision of a just order, a truly good society, it is almost inevitable that this person will soon be wallowing in the mire of selfish ambition. Then political struggle becomes nothing more than using the issues and the needs of society to help assure one's political survival, build one's political power, and savor the joy of victory.

But when politics has been redeemed by being brought under the Lordship of Jesus Christ, one's political struggles are focused and directed by one's tenacious drive for a more just order. This is the standard, not one's selfish ambitions. It is a struggle—often an exhausting, frustrating, debilitating struggle, but one with a goal firmly rooted in moving society toward greater justice. In the process one becomes a servant of those suffering injustice.

This does not mean that one should ignore how one's actions and stands affect one's political power and standing. Christian politics does not necessarily mean one should squander all of one's political influence pursuing clearly nonattainable goals (although at times our Lord may call us to do exactly that). We are called to be wise, perhaps even wily, but whatever wisdom, political influence, and stratagems we have are to be used not to advance ourselves, not to gain more power for power's sake, but to advance God's cause of greater justice in our society. This is the essence of political servanthood.

Thus politics first of all involves struggle and conflict, and developing and using the strategies, plans, and power that go along with struggle. But in its redeemed state, politics as combat centers on the goal of justice and avoids the macho-influenced, selfish, ambition-oriented nature of unredeemed politics.

POLITICS AS COMPROMISE

A second basic characteristic of politics, one closely related to the first, is compromise. It plays a crucial role in politics because it is the means by which individuals or groups that clash are able to resolve their differences and reach agreement. The parties in a dispute meet, find the common ground shared by their conflicting positions, and then agree to support the compromise based on it.

It is clear that when individuals or groups disagree there can be only three possible outcomes: (1) one side or the other wins a clear-cut victory and gets exactly what it wanted; (2) no agreement is reached and a deadlock results; or (3) the two sides reach some sort of a negotiated compromise in which each gets some—but not all—of what it wanted. In politics I have found that the first situation rarely occurs—the latter two are more likely to result. Thus for most practical purposes the choice is deadlock or compromise.

For Christians, who have been taught to struggle for the clear, absolute truth of the Bible, the very word "compromise" has a somewhat unsavory ring to it. In a struggle of justice against injustice, isn't any compromise an unacceptable accommodation to evil? I would say no. I can easily picture various compromises made under certain conditions that would be completely compatible with redeemed politics. In fact, it can be argued that politics based on negotiated compromises is preferable to politics based on one side or the other winning a total victory.

One must not picture the political arena as involving the struggle of absolute good versus absolute evil, of total justice versus total injustice. The real world is never that simple. Typically, even the Christian politician fully committed to pursuing justice in a sinful world feels caught in a dense fog. He or she recognizes some landmarks and has a good sense of the general direction in which to go, but at any given point cannot be completely certain what the next step should be.

Similarly, the public official fully committed to God's truth will have a fairly good sense of justice and what it means on the contemporary scene. But as we saw in the previous chapter, public officials never deal directly with abstract concepts of justice, fairness, and righteousness. The questions they face come in specific, concrete, often technical forms. In such situations— with important information missing and values clashing—even the Christian public official will be able to get only a partial idea of what is needed. And then he or she may be mistaken.

Sometimes Christians who have entered the political arena have had a very rigid, explicit vision of what they believe needs to be accomplished. And they have pursued that vision with a self-confidence that has become arrogance. This is wrong. One mark of Christians in politics should be a sensitivity to their own limitations and fallibility. God's Word is truth. The principle of justice is absolute. But our applications of God's truth and of his standard of justice are often fumbling and shrouded in the fog produced by extremely complex situations, missing information, and the pressures of limited time.

What does all this have to do with compromise? Simply this: when one is asked to compromise, one is not being asked to compromise absolute principles of right and wrong. Instead, one is being asked to compromise on groping, uncertain applications of basic biblical principles. There is a big difference.

As a state senator I was the sponsor of drunk-driving reform legislation in Michigan. In order to get the bills through the Senate, I had to take out one of the key provisions: allowing the police to set up checkpoints at random and to give every driver passing by a sobriety test. Then in the House Judiciary Committee I had to give way on mandatory prison terms for convicted drunk drivers—even for drunk drivers who had killed another person. But much was left in the bills, including long-term, mandatory revocation of the licenses of convicted drunk drivers and stronger enforcement tools for the police and prosecutors. Some criticized me for giving away too much, but I defended what I did on two grounds. One was that if I had held firm I probably would not have gotten any bills passed at all. I was operating according to the "half a loaf is better than none" philosophy, and I believe it is appropriate. One pushes constantly, insistently for more just policies, but progress comes step by step instead of in one fell swoop. As soon as one step is taken, one begins exerting pressure for the next. No bill, no action is seen as the end of the matter. One grabs as much justice as one can today, and comes back for more tomorrow.

But I also justify this approach on a second ground: this step-by-step evolution of policies is less likely to lead to unanticipated, negative consequences. That quantum leap into the future that I may think will usher in the ultimate in justice may, if I could attain it, prove to be a disaster—or at least much less than the vision of true justice I had in mind. Thus the more cautious step-by-step approach that the realities of politics usually force us to take is really not all bad. There is something to be said for giving the police some additional tools with which to deal with drunk drivers, assessing their effectiveness, and then deciding whether or not sobriety checkpoints and mandatory prison terms are also needed. I still think they would prove an important deterrent, but the more guarded approach I was forced to take has its good points.

The compromising nature of politics gets one into trouble when one is really not concerned with issues at all but is only interested in his or her selfish ambitions. Then a person will often be willing to compromise to the point that very little—if any—progress is made. One's chief concern is just to get another bill passed, with the illusion of progress to his or her credit. Sometimes the sponsor of a bill and opposing interests can both get their way. The bill is so radically changed that it really does not accomplish anything anymore. Thus those opposed to the bill get what they want: the status quo is preserved. But the sponsor of the bill gets what he or she wants as well: the passage of a bill "solving" a crucial problem that he or she can advertise in news releases and take credit for in the literature of the next election campaign. Others have often privately urged me to vote for a bill by admitting, "Look, it really isn't going to change anything, anyway."

Under such circumstances compromise is used not to push for as much justice as one can get at that time but to satisfy one's own selfish desires. Justice has become irrelevant, displaced by personal ambition and pride.

In summary, negotiated compromise is a frequent outcome of political combat. In its redeemed form, politics as compromise works insistently, persistently for increased justice in a step-by-step fashion, recognizing that some progress toward greater justice is better than none at all, and that small, incremental steps toward justice may be a wiser stride than giant quantum leaps, which run the danger of going down false paths. But in its unredeemed form, compromise is used to give the illusion of progress or change merely to build up one's reputation and to feed one's selfish ambitions.

POLITICS AS TEAMWORK

A third basic characteristic of politics is teamwork. Working for greater justice through political action is not an individual enterprise but a joint or group process. No one is elected alone, no one gets a bill passed alone, and no one raises the public's consciousness concerning an issue alone. Whoever says "politics" says "teamwork." Almost any political project one can undertake involves building a coalition among like-minded individuals and groups.

Saying this much appears to be stating the obvious. Yet many of the most difficult moral dilemmas and, I suspect, much of the unsavory reputation of politics arise from this very characteristic. The suspicion—and in fact the very real danger— is that in allying oneself with certain individuals and groups one will incur debts that will compromise one's basic independence and integrity.

To get elected, for example, a legislator may rely very heavily upon the local chamber of commerce, a small-business federation, the Right-to-Life organization, several neighborhood associations, and the members of an environmental group. They form the bedrock of his support. They are the ones to whom he turns for campaign funds and volunteers and for help in getting legislation passed. Sometimes he works and cooperates with other groups, but these are the heart of his support—they are his coalition. Without them he could not achieve political success.

All elected officials have a coalition of support groups of this nature. They will vary greatly depending on the background, political philosophy, and partisanship of the individual, but all elected officials are backed by certain coalitions or "teams." Even judges and members of the executive branch usually have certain individuals and groups with whom they identify and to whom they look for advice, encouragement, and support.

But this relationship between public official and supporting coalition cannot be simply a one-way street. One cannot expect individuals and groups to be at one's beck and call, ready and eager to offer support and help, without their in turn having a say about what one is doing. Sometimes even the conscientious, justice-oriented official votes or acts differently or alters the strategies he or she pursues out of deference to one or more groups or individuals.

The Right-to-Life organization is one group that I have worked with very closely throughout my political career. It is part of my coalition or team. Once this relationship resulted in my leading the struggle in the Senate for a bill to forbid the spending of tax money to pay for Medicaid abortions, even though I would have preferred to accomplish this by other means. I thought we should have tried to discharge the committee that had bottled up this legislation. But the majority leader of the Senate opposed this, and the consensus of the Right-to-Life leadership was to insert the desired language in another bill that was in another committee more favorable to our position. The only problem was that doing so probably violated Senate rules in that one could question—to say the least—whether the new language was germane to the intent of the original bill. We had the votes, so we pushed the new language through by overturning a ruling of irrelevancy by the Lieutenant-Governor. I ended up in the uncomfortable position of having to argue on the floor of the Senate and to the news media that something was germane when I and everyone else knew it probably should not be considered germane according to past Senate decisions. Yet I did so, and I still believe I did the right thing, because the team that I had joined, the coalition that I was a part of, had jointly decided that this was the way to go. A politician is not a prima donna but a player in an orchestra.

There are, I believe, two key requirements that a politician must meet to avoid slipping into practicing unredeemed politics, to be able to transform the team aspect of political activity. First of all, the individuals and groups with which one allies oneself must be ones whose basic principles and basic orientations on issues are in keeping with the promotion of a more just order. Politicians guided by selfish ambition will select teams or coalitions based on who will add most to their clout. One will look for groups and individuals with money, prestige, and connections. Robert Caro's biography of Lyndon Johnson's early years, *The Path to Power* (Knopf, 1982), is a sad tale of a person whose every decision, every political alliance seems to have been devoid of any principles or concerns about issues. He judged his associations by a single criterion: will this person or group add to my political power? Can he or it advance my political career? Such politics is unredeemed.

A second requirement is that one must place strict limits on the extent to which one will modify one's positions or tactics to accommodate a group decision that one does not fully agree with. In the situation described earlier I was willing to fight for a germaneness ruling that I knew was probably not in keeping with Senate rules and precedent. But I would not have been willing to fight for a ruling that I felt would be contrary to the state constitution or basic justice. It was a matter of Senate rules, not constitutional provisions or justice.

Yet those who practice unredeemed politics put such a strong emphasis on their personal ambitions that they would not risk losing a key person or group of their coalition by refusing to go along, even if they disagreed with the position on a crucial, fundamental issue. They are no longer team members, parts of coalitions; they are prostitutes. They have sold themselves to their supporters. They ask no questions, but do as they are told.

Especially with the increasing role of big money in American politics, there is a growing tendency for many elected officials to be heavily in debt to certain special-interest groups. Senatorial campaigns often run into the millions of dollars, congressional campaigns into the hundreds of thousands. In 1982 Senator Pete Wilson of California spent $5.1 million winning his race, and in Tennessee's fourth district the Republican and Democratic candidates spent a total of $1.5 million. Jane Byrne spent some $10 million on her futile bid for reelection as mayor of Chicago in 1983. To raise such sums of money, people in politics too often ask, "Who has big money? I'll align myself and my stands on issues with them." This is the wrong approach. Instead one should ask, "Given who I am and what my positions on issues are, who is likely to contribute to my campaign?"

In summary, politics means teamwork, and teamwork means working with others and even modifying one's own positions to maintain the unity of one's team. But in its unredeemed form this is done only with an eye to enhancing one's own selfish ambitions. If it is to be redeemed, political teamwork must occur in the context of working with others who share one's ideals and within boundaries that strictly limit the degree to which one will modify one's positions in deference to these supporters.

POLITICS AS PUBLIC RELATIONS

Anyone in politics—and especially an elected officeholder —is under constant pressure to please and to look good to the public and to key individuals and groups, including the news media. This is important for one's reelection. But it is also important for less obvious but equally significant reasons. Life is easier and one's political influence is greater when it is clear that one is very popular with the media, key individuals and groups, one's own supporters, and the general public. Psychologically, we all need the reassurance that we are OK, that we are good people doing a good job, and we all cringe when we are ridiculed or criticized. Politicians are certainly no exception.

Thus politically active people are under constant pressure to be sensitive to their public relations, to strive not only to do a good job but to take steps to assure that the general public, the news media, and their friends and supporters will all realize what kind of job they are doing.

In its unredeemed form this characteristic of politics can turn politics into nothing more than one big con game. Politics often takes place on two quite separate tracks. One track is the real world of political action, negotiations, and agreements, a world governed by people's values, the realities of the world as it is, powerful interest groups, and powerful political figures. The other track is the world of appearances, of public profiles and rhetoric. Very often the two are quite different.

I recall one occasion when a difficult vote for a tax increase was being discussed in a closed party-caucus, and the party leader explicitly told colleagues who had won election by narrow margins that he did not want them to vote for the increase. Those from electorally "safe" districts were the ones expected to provide the needed votes. I recall the Speaker of the House explicitly telling a representative who was facing a tough reelection fight, "Look, Paul, I'll come over and break your arm if you try to vote for this. We'll get our votes without you." When this happens, how one votes is divorced from what one actually believes about the issue.

I once was facing the question of whether or not to vote for a gasoline-tax increase six weeks before an election that was going to be extremely close. At one point one of the leaders in the fight for the increase told me, "Steve, I think we have enough votes without you. I know you're in a tough election fight. Just vote no. We'll understand. If we should need your vote, I'll let you know."

The more I thought about this the more uncomfortable I became. I was in favor of the tax. It was clearly needed, and the benefits for public transportation were especially great. By voting no I would be giving the impression that I was against the tax, although I and a few others would have known that if my vote had really been needed to pass the tax, it would have been yes. Under those circumstances I concluded that a no vote would have been a lie. I told the leaders of the fight for the tax increase that I was voting yes whether or not they needed my vote. Yet this type of lying, this type of con game, is as common in any legislative chamber as sand in a desert.

A clear example of this type of flimflam occurred once when we in Michigan had to make significant cuts in our state budget because of falling revenues. These cuts were to be made by the Governor and jointly by the Appropriations Committees of the House and Senate. I chaired the Social Services Subcommittee of the Senate Appropriations Committee and thus was deeply involved in making cuts in the social services budget. We were given a target figure we had to reach. After a lot of juggling we figured out a way to make the necessary cuts without having to cut the basic Aid to Families with Dependent Children (AFDC) grants, which in terms of purchasing power had already shrunk by about 25 percent due to inflation and some earlier cuts. But certain committee members objected strenuously. They wanted to see welfare grants cut. People back home were angry and they were not going to be satisfied unless these grants were reduced. Other legislators and I refused to do this—it was unnecessary, and we couldn't imagine how mothers and young children were living on the meager grants they were currently receiving. There was an unbreakable deadlock.

But the seemingly impossible was easily accomplished when we agreed to cut the basic AFDC grants by five percent but to increase by the same amount the supplemental energy grants welfare recipients were receiving. Those legislators insisting that welfare grants be cut could go home and take credit for reducing them by five percent, even though they and everyone else acquainted with the inner workings of the welfare system knew that no welfare recipient was going to receive a penny less in actual money. Those working to cut grants were really not interested in seeing that less money was actually spent; they were only interested in being able to claim that they had reduced welfare grants.

Typically, the worst time for these sorts of flimflam games is during election campaigns. Often the operating procedure seems to be, "Say whatever will get you a few more votes. No one will notice whether or not what you are saying back home squares with the way you vote in Washington or the state capitol."

But I am convinced that politics does not have to operate on this sort of two-track system, that it does not have to be a big con game. But it takes the transforming power of Jesus Christ to say no to this kind of politics. Working to maintain good public relations can be a proper characteristic of politics. The political struggle in a democracy is and should be waged in the glare of publicity. It is a struggle that takes place in public and one on which the public must periodically pass judgment. This means that even Christian politicians must be concerned about their public relations, about their images and how people and the media are perceiving their actions. But the Christian politician, if he or she is to be faithful to the Lord, must completely reject the con-game aspect of politics. The image he or she projects— the public stances taken and the public appearances made— simply must be an accurate reflection of what he or she really is and is really doing. Honesty is the key term here. That must be the inviolable standard. Nothing less will do.

But one cannot assume that simply doing right will automatically ensure that the public will perceive one favorably. Two factors are involved here. First, one has to communicate to the public who one is and what one stands for. Somehow one has to dramatize this or use certain symbols to get this across. It is easy for a politician to portray an opponent as someone he or she is not, and for the public to assume that this is true. At various times in my political career I have been accused of being soft on crime, being in league with the pornography industry, accepting illegal campaign contributions, and being opposed to nonpublic Christian schools. All of these charges are false, but unless one has some means to respond to such charges or has over the years built up quite a different image, one could soon become the victim of such charges.

A second factor is that one is periodically in a situation where he or she will have to take an unpopular stance. Through good public relations one can, so to speak, build up capital that can be drawn upon when one has to take a stance that promotes justice but is nonetheless unpopular. One can also minimize the damage done in this situation by stressing whatever positive factors—from the public's point of view—there may be in this stance.

In summary, politics as public relations grows out of the open, public nature of the political process. In its unredeemed form, politics as public relations degenerates into a big con game marked by attempts to deceive the public into seeing one's actions as something other than what they really are. In its redeemed state, politics as public relations accurately reflects who one is and what one is doing, but does so in such a way that one's public image is improved.

POLITICS AS REPRESENTATION

The United States is ruled by a representative form of government. Under most circumstances the people do not make public-policy decisions directly; they elect representatives who make these decisions. The members of Congress's lower house and of the lower houses of most state legislatures are called representatives. Whom are they representing? Presumably not themselves, not their own ideas of right and wrong, but the people who have elected them.

This concept of governing creates a problem, perhaps even a dilemma, for the Christian who has entered government in order to work for a biblical concept of justice. What happens when a majority of the people who elected a representative are clearly in favor of an unjust policy? One is supposed to represent them—this is a cornerstone of the system of democratic government. Yet one entered politics in order to pursue justice. It is one's vision of a more just social order, an order in which more of God's children have a full opportunity to live free, creative, joyful lives, that has compelled one to make the sacrifices necessary to win public office. Is this to be sacrificed when fifty-one percent of one's constituents take an opposite position? Presumably not. But if one does not do so, hasn't he or she supplanted democracy with an elitism that assumes that the politician knows better than the people who elected him or her?

Before suggesting an answer to these questions, I should point out a crucial factor. The dilemma as posed in the previous paragraph made three assumptions, all of which are false: that all people have opinions on key public-policy issues, that those opinions are known to public-policy makers, and that the intensity with which people hold an opinion and the knowledge on which they base it ought not to affect the policymaker.

In fact, on most public-policy issues a majority of the public will have either no opinion at all or a lightly held, ever-shifting opinion. Public-opinion polls have found that on issues that have not been dominating the news for months—that is, on 99 percent of the issues—even slight differences of wording in the questions can result in big differences in the public's responses. On most issues there is likely to be something like 20 percent on one side, 15 percent on the other, and 65 percent undecided or uncaring. A week later, after a series of news stories on the issue, the 20 percent may have grown to 35 percent and the 15 percent to 40 percent, and the undecided may have shrunk to 25 percent. What does representing the public mean in situations like this? To go with whatever the plurality of the public believes, even if that means shifting one's position from week to week? Presumably not.

Adding to the difficulty is that one can never be certain exactly what the state of opinions back home is on any given issue. Legislators receive letters from their constituents, and some phone calls. In addition, they meet frequently with constituent groups, and their friends feel free to give their opinions after church, at Little League ball games, and at the grocery store. There are periodic public-opinion polls on key issues, but almost invariably they encompass larger areas than one's legislative district. From all this one can get a fuzzy notion of what people back home are thinking. But add this to the shifting, uncertain nature of public opinions themselves, and even the representative determined to reflect accurately whatever the hometown public is thinking is usually left in a thick fog.

Adding still more to the confusion and uncertainty is the factor of intensity. What if 60 percent of the people (we will assume perfect knowledge here) favor one side of an issue, but favor it in a lukewarm manner, without much knowledge or strong feelings about the issue. And 20 percent of the people believe the opposite way but feel very intensely about the issue. To them it is one of the key issues facing our nation; they know the issue well and have very strong feelings about it. The other 20 percent of the public has no opinion at all. Should the legislator who is trying faithfully to reflect the public's feelings side with the marginally committed 60 percent or the intensely committed 20 percent? Abstract theories of representation have no answer. A clear majority is on one side. If it is a simple matter of majority rule—of counting noses and going with whatever side is larger—the answer is clear. But ought not both the strength of one's opinion and the amount of knowledge on which it is based count for something? The 20 percent, because of the strength of their beliefs, are probably writing many more letters, meeting with their representatives, and in other ways expressing their opinions, while the 60 percent are largely sitting back, uninvolved.

This in fact is precisely the situation that exists in regard to gun-control legislation. Public-opinion polls regularly show a clear majority of Americans in favor of stricter gun-control legislation. But the minority that is opposed to further gun control believes in its position much more strongly and is much more willing to act on its beliefs than is the majority that favors stricter gun controls. In my years of political campaigning I have been asked about my position on gun-control legislation dozens of times, and only one time did the questioner turn out to be someone who favored stricter gun controls. All the other questioners were people strongly opposed to further gun controls. If I were seeking merely to reflect the opinions of the people I represent, should I be for or against further gun control?

With this muddled picture and these unanswered questions in mind, let us turn to the meaning of politics as representation.

In its unredeemed form, politics as representation is again guided by one's selfish ambitions. The question is how one can use or manipulate public opinions to maximize one's chances of election or reelection and to increase one's political power. Thus one will naturally avoid going against strongly held public opinions. Intensity becomes the key factor. Only people who feel intensely about an issue are likely to vote for or against a legislator at the next election depending on his or her position on that issue, or are likely to write a nasty letter to the editorial column of the local newspaper if the legislator takes the "wrong" position. Special weight will also be given to the opinions of past or potential campaign contributors or powerful people in the community.

What must also be factored in is potential intensity. An issue may be attracting very little attention; apathy may be dominant. But the issue is such that an opponent can use it in the next election to make one look bad in the eyes of many voters. Perhaps it is an issue that an opponent might use to make one look as though he or she is "soft on crime," against helping needy senior citizens, against education, or in favor of wasteful welfare programs. The person guided by selfish ambitions will also be very sensitive to such issues.

Thus, in unredeemed politics, the politician is constantly on the alert for issues that may draw strong positive or negative reactions from the public, using these issues to build support or avoid losses and justifying these actions on the basis of representing the people. But the principal motivator here is really selfish ambition, a desire to strengthen or solidify one's political base.

In redeemed politics one follows one's conception of justice, not the leanings of public opinions. If a Christian, justice-oriented legislator is convinced on a clear issue of justice that even the overwhelming majority of people are on the wrong side, he or she should go against the wishes of that majority and support the side of justice. To do otherwise would negate the entire point of having a justice-oriented Christian in public office. The reason for holding public office is betrayed by the Christian official who abandons justice as soon as the majority seems to favor a position that doesn't support a more just order. Each vote and each position a justice-oriented legislator takes should be saying, "This is what I believe is right and just," not "This is what I believe most people in my district are in favor of."

But more needs to be said. The Christian legislator can easily fall victim to an arrogant elitism in which the prevailing attitude is, "Look, I know what's best for you. So you just be quiet and accept what I know is right. After all, I'm following biblical justice." Such an attitude is wrong and would set redeemed, justice-oriented politics at odds with democratic politics.

What needs to be added is, first of all, a strong sense of Christian humility based on an understanding of one's own fallibility and limited knowledge. The Christian legislator should vote according to his or her own convictions of justice, even if constituents overwhelmingly oppose that position. But whenever Christian legislators find themselves in this situation, the first question that arises is, "What am I missing that so many others are seeing?"

There is an old Indian proverb that one should not criticize another until one has walked in the other's moccasins. Similarly, a public official should not vote on an issue deeply affecting other people until he or she has walked in their shoes, has spent time with them, learned from them, and genuinely tried to understand their perspective. Policymakers who are true servants of those whom they represent will act only after walking and talking open-mindedly with those for whom they are making decisions. Sometimes doing so will make them change their minds. When policymakers take this servantlike attitude, justice-oriented politics is saved from degenerating into an arrogant, elitist politics. True representation still exists.

A second factor that must be mentioned is that the representation process should not be a simple one-way street, with the public telling their representative how to vote and then he or she dutifully obeying these marching orders. In redeemed politics the representation process is a creative, two-way street. Constituents can often help educate and broaden the perspective and knowledge of their representative, but we shouldn't forget that the representative can do the same for those whom he or she represents. Through personal meetings, telephone conversations, responses to letters, and statements to the media, legislators are able to share with their constituents what they have been able to learn in Washington or the state capitol. Citizens and citizen groups tend to see things only from a particular perspective, one that is often narrow. The legislator, on the other hand, is forced to view things from a much broader perspective, and thus has a responsibility to share that perspective with his or her constituents. A valuable two-way communications system is thereby created.

Politics as representation is important. Christian, justice-oriented public officials are representatives. But this does not mean that they slavishly follow the shifts in public opinion, and surely it does not mean that they put selfish ambition first by reducing the representation process to no more than trying to pacify people with strong opinions, to head off possible adverse public reactions, or to otherwise solidify their political base. Instead, Christian public officials redeem the political process by pursuing justice, but they allow their vision of what is just in a specific setting to be informed by the views and knowledge of the people they represent. They take the time to dialogue with those whom they represent, and are willing both to lead and to be led by them.

Politics that is enslaved to the powers of this dark world and politics that has been redeemed by Jesus Christ differ widely because they follow two entirely different standards. The politics of this world are based on selfish ambitions. Getting ahead, building one's political power, expanding one's base—this is what politics is all about. One first takes care of number one and only then allows other goals and values into one's calculations (although there are some public officials who never get past number one!). The politics of our Lord is based on servanthood and justice. Justice is the goal, and as one subordinates personal needs and desires to pursue that goal, one becomes a servant.

All that we have said in this chapter concerning the redeemed and unredeemed manifestations of politics—politics as combat, compromise, teamwork, public relations, and representation—flows from this crucial distinction.

5

THE OPTIONS FOR
POLITICAL INVOLVEMENT

Throughout this book I have frequently written of political involvement as though it were a single, simple thing that everyone knows and recognizes. Now it is time to be more specific, to explore the variety of activities that constitute political involvement. Christians should—indeed, must—be politically involved, but that involvement can take many different forms.

This last chapter gives guidance to the concerned Christian who may not know exactly how to go about influencing the political system. To many people, government and politics seem enormously complicated, ponderous, and impenetrable; and they feel small, weak, and alone. But it doesn't have to be this way. Citizens concerned with justice—acting alone or, better yet, together—can have an impact on today's politics and public policies. Making an impact may not always be easy, and it may be done in less well-known, less glamorous forums than one might initially imagine. But with time and effort citizens can have a real and significant impact on public policies.

Three basic factors need to be kept in mind as one approaches the question of political involvement. The first is that in a free, open democracy such as the United States there is no escaping political involvement. The person who refuses to be actively involved in politics in any way, refusing even to vote, nevertheless has a political impact. Such inaction increases the influence of others who participate and tends to reinforce the status quo—to support existing policies and personalities. In short, both participation and nonparticipation have political consequences. The only question is will that impact—no matter how large or how small—be good or bad.

A second factor to remember is that the American system of government is a very decentralized, open system. When considering political involvement one should not necessarily start out thinking of the White House, Congress, and Washington, D. C. These are important, of course, and I am sure God is calling certain Christians to be deeply and actively involved in seeking to turn those institutions toward greater justice. But one should also think of state legislatures, city or county governing bodies, and local boards and commissions. Many crucial decisions about justice are made on the state and local levels, and power is typically even more decentralized on these levels than it is on the national level. Numerous citizen boards and commissions are deeply involved in issues of land use and zoning, education, transportation (especially roads and highways), and social welfare. All of these groups frequently grapple directly with issues that have serious implications for justice. Part of being a servant is a willingness to work hard at unglamorous jobs far removed from the spotlight of publicity.

A third factor that has repeatedly impressed me as I have dealt with and been involved in the political system is the degree to which it is open to and penetrable by the person willing to spend time and effort seeking influence. The decentralized nature of the political system, combined with the all-too-prevalent apathy of the public, produces a situation where people willing to be involved can soon have a greater influence than they ever expected to have. Often the problem is finding enough citizens willing to fill the many positions on local or state boards and commissions. Positions in both political parties often go vacant because the parties can find no one willing to take on the job. Candidates frequently face no opposition in an election because the opposing party was unable to find anyone willing to run. An acquaintance of mine moved to a new city when he was starting out as an attorney. Since he was a Democrat, he called the local Democratic chairman to offer his services. He thought he might be asked to stuff envelopes and do a little canvassing.

Instead, the chairman called him a couple of days later and asked if he would be willing to run for Congress because the party was having trouble finding a candidate!

The point in all this is not that one's attempts to build political influence in a certain area will always be successful; indeed, sometimes people will be strongly opposed by the establishment, which sees them as threats to its power. But the person who is willing to start out small and get involved in an area that may not be the most obvious, visible aspect of government can quickly build his or her political influence to the point where he or she can be used by God to bring about a more just order.

But I need to specify more clearly the different levels and forms of political involvement and how to go about becoming involved. In the remaining portion of this chapter I consider political involvement at three different levels, and the form it takes at each one.

THE CITIZEN PARTICIPANT

Not every Christian should be expected to be deeply and actively involved in politics. Gifts differ and callings differ. Christ's body has many different members, each with its assigned tasks. But every Christian should at least be a citizen participant.

A citizen participant tries to maintain at least general knowledge of political affairs and candidates, votes regularly, and occasionally expresses his or her opinions on political issues by writing political officials, signing petitions, or attending meetings about public policy. He or she will also belong to one or two groups with a political agenda.

Being a good citizen participant begins with a commitment to staying generally informed about politics. I would not suggest that every person needs to spend hours each week learning the details of events in Congress, all aspects of the latest international conflict, the contents of alternative state-tax proposals, or the details of a local zoning dispute. But all of us should at least know the names of the state, national, and local elected officials who represent us, and have a general knowledge of the key issues being debated on national, state, and local levels. Spending an hour each week with a national news magazine such as *Time* or *Newsweek*, watching a television news program once or twice a week, and glancing through the local newspaper would be enough to maintain this level of knowledge.

This much is necessary to be a true citizen, to be able to relate to and participate in the free, open government that God has given the United States. To be a participating Christian citizen one must have opinions based on knowledge, and then try to move government toward the God-ordained goal of increased justice. Without even a broad, general knowledge of political events one must either be guided blindly by others or absolve oneself from any participation in government. Then one might just as well be living in the Soviet Union or in a repressive society like Guatemala. People who abdicate their political roles in this way are merely going along for the ride. For us as Christians to do so is to say that we care nothing for the means God has given us to restrain evil and to promote justice, or for those who desperately need the more just order only government can bring.

If, on the other hand, one is at least minimally informed, one is then in a position to express one's opinions by voting and other means. With thousands—often even millions—of others participating in an election, the influence any single person has seems to be so minimal that one is constantly tempted not to bother to vote. Admittedly, it is foolish for anyone to believe that his or her vote alone will be used by God to usher in his just order. But the collective impact voters can have is crucial. People should think in terms of the impact their combined votes have, and then vote because they recognize their God-given, democratic duty to add their small parts to the whole. To recognize the collective impact of voting, one only has to imagine the result if all justice-oriented, Christian citizens would no longer vote. The forces of injustice and selfishness would make huge gains.

Participating citizens will also avail themselves of other opportunities to influence the political system. Examples abound: signing a petition being circulated at church or one's place of work, writing to a public official, or attending a meeting called to educate the public on a particular issue or to call for change

86

in a public policy. The point is not that every Christian citizen should be constantly writing and attending meetings to fulfill his or her obligations as a citizen, but that once or twice a year, when an issue of special concern or importance comes up, he or she should be prepared to express those opinions in support of more justice in society.

The final obligation of the Christian citizen participant is to belong to one or two groups that are politically involved to some degree. If one stays even generally informed on public-policy issues, he or she is likely to become particularly interested in one or two of them. The easiest and most efficient way to keep track of what is happening on an issue is to join a group with special interests in that area. What I have in mind are groups that, for example, are associated with one's profession or place of employment, such as a labor union, an educators' organization, or a professional society—or it could be an advocacy group such as Right to Life, Amnesty International, or the League of Conservation Voters. There are also many politically oriented groups, such as Bread for the World and the Association for Public Justice, that have a strong Christian foundation. The examples could be multiplied, whatever one's area of chief concern—abortion, environmental protection, consumer protection, neighborhoods, civil rights, nuclear warfare, social-welfare policies, or business regulation.

Joining one or two politically oriented groups is crucial. Joining a group takes only a few minutes' time and usually costs no more than $10 to $30 a year. Yet I suspect that the single biggest destroyer of well-intended efforts to influence the government for good is the failure to do this relatively simple thing. Let me explain.

It is difficult to achieve effective citizen influence partly because of the very complexity of government in the United States. The three levels of government—national, state, and local—usually deal in some fashion with most public-policy issues. Each level of government is divided into executive, legislative, and judicial branches, although on the local level the executive and legislative roles are sometimes combined. Both Congress and the state legislatures (except for that of Nebraska) are divided into two separate houses, and each house is divided into numerous committees and subcommittees.

Because of these complexities, many citizen attempts to influence the system go awry. Sometimes the right push goes in the wrong direction. State legislators will receive letters urging them to vote a certain way on issues that are before the United States Congress. And United States Congressmen will receive letters urging them to vote a certain way on state-legislative issues. In addition, letters to legislators will often fail to have their intended impact because their timing is wrong. Legislators often receive letters urging support of or opposition to measures that have come before them weeks earlier.

Another problem is that, because of the complexities of the legislative process, people running for reelection can often fool voters into thinking they were on one side of an issue even though they were really on the other. There are numerous committee votes and usually votes on many amendments before the vote on the final passage of a measure. A legislator can vote against a bill in committee and vote for every weakening amendment that is proposed, but then vote in favor of the bill on final passage and take credit for supporting the bill and its objectives. Or he or she can vote for the bill and then vote against overturning a presidential or gubernatorial veto, yet take credit for supporting the bill.

One's best protection against errors of these types is to join a group that deals with the issue or issues that one is most concerned about. The group will have paid staff members whose full-time job is to understand the issues at stake, understand the legislative, executive, and judicial processes, and keep the membership informed about what is happening on the issues. Most groups, for example, inform their members when a crucial vote is coming up in one of the houses of the legislature and urge them to write letters at that time. Most groups put out annual or biannual voting-charts that give every legislator's votes on ten to twenty issues key to their concerns. This is a much better guide to how legislators are really voting on issues than their own self-serving newsletters or campaign literature.

Joining a group instead of being an added burden makes being an informed, responsible citizen easier and more likely to result in positive, justice-promoting efforts. At the end of this chapter is a list of the addresses of a wide variety of groups, including many groups with a Christian political orientation. One is the Association for Public Justice, an organization of evangelical Christians actively working to inform its members about major public-policy issues from a standpoint of justice and to influence governmental policies on such matters as land conservation, nuclear weapons, and abortion. Similarly, Bread for the World, another group listed, is a Christian organization dedicated to influencing governmental policies that attack the problem of world hunger. It educates its members on hunger issues, provides information on how senators and congressmen are voting on crucial hunger issues, and alerts its members to crucial hunger issues when they come before Congress.

I am convinced that if all thirty million adult evangelicals would take the minimal steps to be citizen participants, their impact would be astounding. They would become an active, informed force, courted by every politician in both political parties.

THE CITIZEN ACTIVIST

Not all Christians are called by God to go beyond being citizen participants and become citizen activists—but some are. And those who are play a crucial role in making possible the political impact of the broader church of Jesus Christ. God calls his church to pursue political justice. Christian citizen activists play a significant part in the church's ability to do so.

The citizen activist moves beyond the political involvements of the citizen participant by playing an active role in politically oriented groups, political parties, or candidates' campaign organizations. (They do not, however, have full-time, paid positions or hold public office themselves.) A citizen activist may be deeply involved in an association or organization with a political agenda. This is the person who serves as an officer in the local Right-to-Life organization or on the board of the Sierra Club, or who volunteers to help get out a mailing for a nuclear-disarmament group.

Previously I emphasized the key role political advocacy groups play in keeping their members informed and in directing the political energies of their members. What needs to be equally emphasized is the tremendous influence groups have in the American political process. Where would the anti-abortion movement be without Right to Life? What would environmental protection be without environmental groups such as the Sierra Club, Environmental Action, and the League of Conservation Voters? Bread for the World has made important headway in dealing with world-hunger problems. Within six years of its founding, a group called FAIR came close to achieving the first major change in the United States' immigration laws in recent history. Within months of opening its Washington office, the Association for Public Justice—the Christian political action and education group I mentioned earlier—was able to help start the process of implementing the Farmland Preservation Policy Act, which had become stalled in the Agriculture Department. Neighborhood associations have time and again moved local governments.

Groups, in short, are crucial to the American way of politics. The system responds much more quickly to pressures from groups than from individuals. And groups, in turn, depend to a large degree on activist members to accomplish their goals. It is extremely important that all Christians express their Christian concern for a more just world in part by joining one or two groups, but it is also important that some Christians move beyond this and become very active, key members of certain groups. There are enough Christians with enough skills and dedication— if they would move in force into groups that are especially active in pursuing justice-related issues—that they could make a dramatic impact on our nation as well as on our states and communities.

More Christians also need to become activists in the electoral process. The two political parties, groups supporting or opposing ballot proposals, and candidates for public office all stand in desperate need of volunteers and contributions. Ultimately, much of American politics comes down to the ballot box: who will hold what public office and what proposals will be approved by the voters. I have seen crucial ballot proposals with very deep and obvious implications for justice—proposals involving environmental protection, criminal justice, and education for handicapped children—being won or lost without significant support from active campaigns—simply because there were no citizens willing to become involved in such campaigns.

Similarly, candidates for public office are almost totally dependent on individual citizens who are willing to give time and money to their campaigns. Having been a candidate for public office many times, I can vouch for their importance—one can go nowhere without them. In most areas of the country and under most circumstances, one's political party will be worth very little in terms of volunteers and campaign funds. It is not unusual for candidates for Congress to spend some $250,000, only $10,000 to $15,000 of which comes from their political party. The rest is raised by their own committees. Typically, good candidates—those who are independent in that they are not aligned with powerful special interests—are in the greatest need of citizen help and support. Yet so few people are willing to become involved in political campaigns that even a few dedicated individuals can make an enormous difference. I know of state legislative races that were won largely because of a group of ten or twelve people who were willing to help ten to twenty hours a week for several weeks.

Political parties are also in chronic need of financial contributions and volunteers. This is a less direct means to effect more just public policies, since both American political parties are very pluralistic, with people on each side of many issues in each party. Thus one's activities in either one of the parties are usually not directly connected with certain desired public-policy outcomes. Nevertheless, it is good to have at least some Christians actively involved in each political party, giving voice to the need for more just policies. In some states —especially in some of the northeastern states—parties still play a major role in nominating candidates and affecting public policies. In those states it is more important for Christians to be active in the two political parties.

The need for citizen activists is so great that getting involved in an organization, a party, or a candidate's campaign is usually not a problem. The bigger problem is how to limit one's commitment to the time or money one is able to give. To become involved in an organization, a person can begin simply by joining the group. For some groups it is necessary to join the local chapter as well as the national organization. It is especially important to join the local chapter if one intends to become actively involved. Then one can attend local meetings of the group, at which there will usually be opportunities to volunteer to serve on certain committees or to take on other tasks. Once a person has volunteered, he or she will probably be asked to undertake more tasks than originally planned.

In most states, political parties have someone occupying a position on the precinct level, usually a precinct committee person or precinct captain. People are either appointed to fill these positions or are elected to them in a primary. They are a good place to start for those interested in being active in a political party. Or one can watch the papers for announcements of party meetings, then attend and volunteer when help is requested. Sometimes it is easier to get involved in an organization of Young Democrats or Young Republicans or in a Republican or Democratic club than in the formal party organizations.

One should also watch for candidates' announcements of their candidacies. Then one can call them and volunteer to help, or can stop by a campaign headquarters and ask for some literature, and, if in agreement with the candidate, offer to help out.

Whatever the form active involvement may take, the Christian citizen activist is playing a crucial role in the pursuit of justice. Without Christian citizen activists willing to expend time, energy, and money to support justice-promoting candidates, groups, and causes, those candidates, groups, and causes—and the justice to which they are dedicated—will be lost.

THE PROFESSIONAL ACTIVIST

The highest level of political involvement is that of the professional activist—that is, the person who holds a public office or a full-time, paid position with a political party or politically oriented group. By choosing either kind of position, one moves beyond the private citizen who is actively involved in politics.

The tremendous importance of the staff members of a politically involved group grows out of the importance of groups in our political system. To be the executive director of a local environmental organization, the receptionist at a Right-to-Life office, or the newsletter editor for an organization against the nuclear arms race—if done for justice and in the name of Christ—is a high calling that can bear enormous fruit in the form of more just public policies. Also important are staff positions with legislators and other elected officials. Full-time, paid positions within a political party can also sometimes offer opportunities to work for greater political justice.

Usually the people who get these positions began by volunteering their help to a group, party, candidate, or office-holder. To be able to make politics a profession, one needs at least to be active in one's community and its groups and organizations. For example, being active in a neighborhood association may lead to job opportunities not only with the neighborhood association but with other groups as well, since the skills needed do not vary much from group to group.

Holding public office is also a possibility to consider. After having stressed the great opportunities to be an influence for good through group, party, or volunteer activities, I must say that the way to have the most direct, immediate, commanding role in influencing public policies is to be the person who is actually forming them. In the final analysis, it is the legislators, the judges, the bureaucrats, and the board or commission members who make the final decisions that lead toward or away from a more just order. Others can be important—sometimes extremely important—to the total process, but in the end it is the officeholders who make the decisions. Thus to aspire to hold public office is to aspire to be God's servants for much good.

When one thinks of holding public office, it is easy to think only of state or national legislative office, and because these are the offices that I have held and/or aspired to, much of this book is oriented toward holding such positions. But there are numerous other public offices that Christians should also consider, many of which are part-time positions. There are local legislative bodies such as city councils, county governing boards, and school boards. There are many boards and commissions—usually appointed—on the state and local levels, such as zoning boards, highway or road commissions, water-quality boards, drainage boards, and on and on. One should also think in terms of judicial offices. In most states certain judges run for election, and others are appointed. There are also court clerks, bailiffs, and probation officers who play important roles. There are prosecutors and others in the prosecutors' offices who also are key people in the system of justice. Then there are the huge executive branches of local, state, and national government. Through appointment or through competitive entrance examinations, people can obtain key positions in which they not only carry out public policies but also help shape them.

The point is that there are almost unlimited opportunities for the concerned Christian—depending on his or her talents, inclinations, education, and time—to become involved in holding public office. Doing so is often not easy. Typically, the work is difficult, the pay low or nonexistent, and the public recognition limited. But the opportunities to be a servant by pursuing justice are almost unlimited.

The need is not simply for a handful of professional activists. By depending on a few such key people, the Christian community runs the risk of committing the "political star" error—of believing that a handful of Christians occupying strategic positions of political leadership—political stars—will be able to make an effective Christian witness. The problem with this belief is that any one public-office holder has only a limited amount of influence. Many Christians who are deeply concerned about justice take great satisfaction in having a person such as Senator Mark Hatfield in high public office. This is appropriate. But I am confident that Senator Hatfield would himself be the first to admit that as an individual he has very limited influence in Washington.

What we need is not an isolated Christian here and there in government, fighting lonely battles for greater justice. What we need is for large numbers of Christians committed to justice to occupy many offices on all levels of government. Each one—no matter how high the office he or she is occupying—will have only limited influence in moving society toward greater justice. But cumulatively the justice they can achieve will "roll on like a river" (Amos 5:24), sweeping away mountains of injustice.

The route to obtaining public office varies greatly. It obviously makes a big difference if one is aspiring to be elected to the United States Senate or seeking appointment to the town library-board. What is most crucial, however, is being an active member of one's community. In doing so one sharpens needed skills and develops contacts and friends who can be called on for help in securing a position in public office. The person who is, for example, an active church member, the president of the local PTA, and a neighborhood-association board member will have the contacts and the record of active civic involvement that will be crucial should he or she decide to run for the state legislature.

At the close of this book I come back to the theme that I began with: pursuing justice in a sinful world. The world is indeed sinful: greed, selfish ambition, disorder, oppression, and exploitation are all too much with us. But God has given us government by which to work for a more just order even in the midst of the bitter fruit produced by humankind's sinfulness. Government, however, can be turned from its God-established purposes of justice and order to oppression and death. It is in the great potential of government for good and for evil that Christians—who weep over despoiled environments, menacing arms races, and exploited poor—find their challenge.

APPENDIX

CITIZEN ORGANIZATIONS CONCERNED
WITH JUSTICE ISSUES

GENERAL

*Association for Public Justice
P. O. Box 19213
Washington, D.C. 20006

*Clergy and Laity Concerned
198 Broadway
New York, New York 10038

Common Cause
2030 M St. N.W.
Washington, D.C. 20036

Congress Watch
215 Pennsylvania Ave. S.E.
Washington, D.C. 20003

*Evangelicals for Social Action
P. O. Box 76560
Washington, D.C. 20013

*Friends Committee on National
Legislation
245 2nd St. N.E.
Washington, D.C. 20013

League of Women Voters
1730 M St. N.W., 10th Floor
Washington, D.C. 20036

M.A.D.D.
(Mothers Against Drunk Drivers)
669 Airport Freeway, Suite 310
Hurst, Texas 76053

---

*An asterisk indicates organizations which, at least broadly speaking, have a Christian outlook or basis.

* Mennonite Central Committee
100 Maryland Ave. N.E.
Washington, D.C. 20002

ABORTION/LIFE ISSUES

* Christian Action Council
422 C St. N.E.
Washington, D.C. 20001

National Right to Life
419 7th St. N.W., Suite 419
Washington, D.C. 20004

AGRICULTURE/LAND RESOURCES CONSERVATION

The Cornucopia Project
33 E. Minor St.
Emmaus, Pennsylvania 18049

National Agriculture Lands Center
400 C St. N.E.
Washington, D.C. 20002

ARMS RACE/NUCLEAR WAR

Coalition for a New Foreign and Military Policy
120 Maryland Ave. N.E.
Washington, D.C. 20002

SANE
711 G St. S.E.
Washington, D.C. 20003

CIVIL RIGHTS/HUMAN RIGHTS

Amnesty International
304 W. 58th St.
New York, New York 10019

NAACP
186 Remsen St.
Brooklyn, New York 11201

APPENDIX

National Urban League
500 E. 62nd St.
New York, New York 10021

CRIMINAL JUSTICE

*Prison Fellowship/Justice Fellowship
P. O. Box 40562
Washington, D.C. 20016

Various professional groups such as the American Bar Association, organizations of prosecuting attorneys, and corrections and judicial associations.

EDUCATION

Association for Retarded Citizens
2501 Avenue J
Arlington, Texas 76011

Citizens for Educational Freedom
854 Washington Building
Washington, D.C. 20005

Local PTAs, various professional organizations such as educators' groups, and school-administrators' and school-board associations.

ENVIRONMENT/ENERGY

Energy Conservation Coalition
1725 I St. N.W., Suite 601
Washington, D.C. 20006

Environmental Action
1346 Connecticut Ave. N.W.
Washington, D.C.

League of Conservation Voters
317 Pennsylvania Ave. S.E.
Washington, D.C. 20003

National Audubon Society
P. O. Box 2666
Boulder, Colorado 80322

Sierra Club
330 Pennsylvania Ave. S.E.
Washington, D.C. 20003

HUNGER

* Bread for the World
6411 Chillum Pl. N.W.
Washington, D.C. 20012

SOCIAL WELFARE

American Association of Retired Persons
1909 K St. N.W.
Washington, D.C. 20049

* Interfaith Action for Economic Justice
110 Maryland Ave. N.E.
Washington, D.C. 20002

National Council of Senior Citizens
925 15th St. N.W.
Washington, D.C. 20005

94880